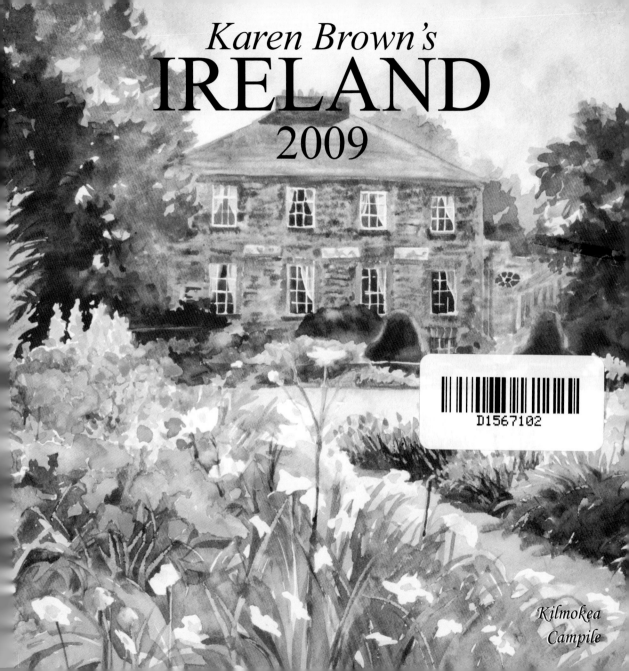

Karen Brown's
IRELAND
2009

D1567102

Kilmokea
Campile

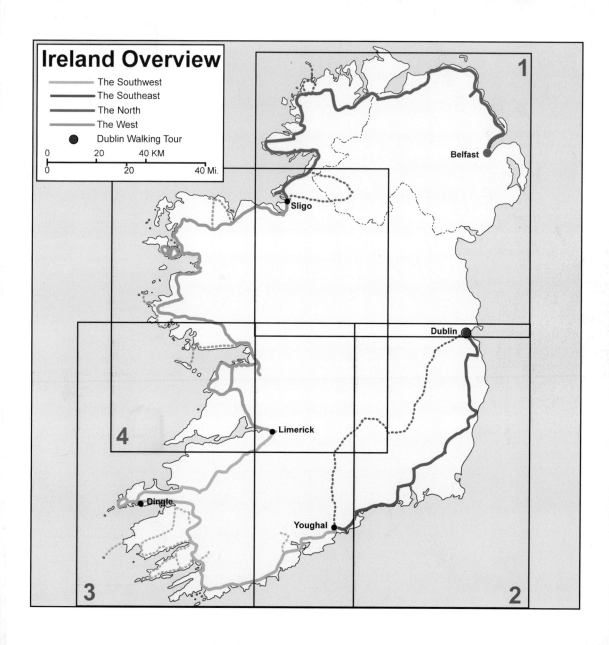

Ireland Overview

- The Southwest
- The Southeast
- The North
- The West
- ● Dublin Walking Tour

0   20   40 KM
0   20   40 Mi.

1

Belfast

Sligo

Dublin

Limerick

4

Dingle

Youghal

3

2

Tory Island

R257

N56

INISHOWEN

Giants Causeway

Ballintoy

Bushmills

Coleraine

A37

A26

Glenariff Nat'l Park

Carnlough

Rathmullen

Ramelton

Lough Foyle

Londonderry

A2

Letterkenny

N13

Glenveagh Nat'l Park

R251

N56

N13

N14

A6

A29

Upperlands

Ballymena

A2

Larne

Finn

N15

A5

Carrick Fergus

Bangor

Ardara

A6

Templepatrick

A26

Holywood

Glencolumbkille

R263

N56

Donegal

A505

A29

Lough Neagh

Belfast

A1

Newtownards

Bruckless

Dunkineely

Omagh

Strangford Lough

Donegal Bay

N3

A32

Dungannon

A3

Magheralin

A24

Ballyshannon

Lower Lough Erne

A46

A4

A4

Enniskillen

Upper Lough Erne

A509

N2

N16

Clones

A3

A28

A1

A2

Lisadell

N15

Drumcliff

Sligo

N59

Cloverhill

N3

Newry

A2

Riverstown

Ballymote

Lough Allen

Kilmactranny

Annagh

N2

N1

Dundalk

Carrick on Shannon

N4

N17

N55

N3

Castlerea

N60

Longford

Lough Sheelin

N63

N55

Inny

N4

Lough Ree

Mullingar

N6

N4

N3

Straffan

Howth

Dublin

Ireland Map 1

- ● Places to Stay
- ── The North
- ── The West
- ⬤ Dublin Walking Tour

0   20   40 KM

0   20   40 Mi.

Ireland Map 2

Contents

Beneta
you live on in the hearts of everyone
you touched and loved while you were here

Cover painting: Kilmokea, Campile.

Author: June Eveleigh Brown.

Editors: Anthony Brown, Clare Brown, Karen Brown, June Eveleigh Brown, Debbie Tokumoto, Melissa Jaworski.

Illustrations: Barbara Maclurcan Tapp.

Cover painting: Jann Pollard.

Front photos: Cork countryside & Gallerus Oratary (keewi.com).

Maps: Rachael Kircher-Randolph.

Technical assistance: Andrew Harris.

Distributed by National Book Network, 15200 NBN Way, Blue Ridge Summit, PA 17214, USA. Tel: 717-794-3800 or 1-800-462-6420, Fax: 1-800-338-4500, Email: custserv@nbnbooks.com

A catalog record for this book is available from the British Library.

ISSN 1535-7341

Introduction

Writers wax lyrical about Ireland's spectacular scenery: ever-changing landscapes, splendid seascapes, purple moorlands, monastic ruins, enchanting lakes, towering fortresses, and vast, spreading patchworks of fields in every shade of green. Believe every word they say, but realize that it's the people with their open friendliness and warmth of welcome that make a visit to Ireland special. This guide is all about Irish hospitality and staying in places where you are a houseguest rather than a customer. Ireland is not conducive to rushing: the narrow country roads lend themselves to exploration at a leisurely pace where you return the smile and wave of greeting of those you pass. Take time to stop at a pub and be drawn into conversation, and when you get lost, ask directions and learn a bit of history or folklore as a bonus, along with the directions.

About This Guide

Karen Brown's Ireland is written specifically for independent travelers who want to experience a slice of Irish life staying as guests in country houses, farms, and family-run hotels. Our guide is not written for those who want the symmetry of worldwide, hotel chains with their identical bathrooms and mini-bars. The fondest memories of a visit to the Emerald Isle are those of its warm-hearted, friendly people, and there can be no better way to meet the Irish than to stay with them in their homes.

The guide includes all types of lodgings ranging from a simple farmhouse bed & breakfast to a luxurious country estate, owned and run by a welcoming family. These are often the kinds of places where you are expected to carry your own bags. Service may not be the most efficient and occasionally the owners have their eccentricities, which all adds to the allure. There are enough recommendations in every price category to enable you to tailor your trip to your budget. We have recommended accommodation in the widest of price ranges, so please do not expect the same standard of luxury at, for example, Foxmount Farm, as The Park Hotel Kenmare—there is no comparison—yet each is outstanding in what it offers. Rates are quoted in euros in the Republic of Ireland and pounds sterling in Northern Ireland.

To keep you on the right track, we have formed itineraries linking the most interesting sightseeing, enabling you to spend from a few weeks to a month exploring this fascinating island. In addition, we have designed a walking tour of Dublin's fair city that blends culture, history, shopping, and Guinness.

Please supplement this book with the Karen Brown website (*www.karenbrown.com*). Our site contains not only a wealth of information for planning your vacation, but also post-press updates on our guides, and is a handy source for Michelin maps. A great many of the properties in this guide are featured there (their web addresses are on their description pages) with photos and direct links to their email and their own website.

About Ireland

The following pointers are given in alphabetical order, not in order of importance.

AIRFARE

Karen Brown's Guides have long recommended Auto Europe for their excellent car rental services. Their air travel division, Destination Europe, an airline broker working with major American and European carriers, offers deeply discounted coach- and business-class fares to over 200 European gateway cities. It also gives Karen Brown travelers an additional 5% discount off its already highly competitive prices (cannot be combined with any other offers or promotions). We recommend making reservations by phone at (800) 835-1555. When phoning, be sure to use the Karen Brown ID number 99006187 to secure your discount.

CLIMATE

It has been said that there is no such thing as climate in Ireland—only weather, and no such thing as bad weather—only the wrong clothes. This is because the changes in conditions from day to day, and even from hour to hour, seem greater than the changes from one season to the next. The Atlantic Ocean and the air masses moving east give Ireland very little seasonal variation in temperature, producing mild winters and cool summers. The ocean's influence is strongest near the coast, especially in winter when areas bordering the sea are milder than those inland. Coastal areas, particularly in the west, also have less variation in temperature between day and night. Even when it rains, and it does, it never pours—it's just soft Irish rain that keeps the isle emerald. The best thing is to be prepared for sun and sudden squalls at all times.

CLOTHING

Ireland is an easygoing place and casual clothes are acceptable everywhere, even at the fanciest restaurants. Because the weather is changeable, layers of sweaters and shirts that can be added to and removed are recommended. A lightweight, waterproof jacket with a hood is indispensable. Do not haul huge suitcases into bed & breakfasts; rather, we suggest that you have a small suitcase (the size that fits under your airline seat) that you take into the places you stay, leaving larger luggage in the car.

CURRENCY

The unit of currency in Northern Ireland is the pound sterling, while in the Republic of Ireland it is the euro. The two currencies do not have equal value. Visit our website (*www.karenbrown.com/news/currency.html*) for an online currency converter.

An increasingly popular and convenient way to obtain foreign currency is simply to use your bankcard at an ATM machine. You pay a fixed fee for this but, depending on the amount you withdraw, it is usually less than the percentage-based fee charged to exchange currency or travelers' checks. Be sure to check with your bank or credit card company about fees and necessary pin numbers prior to departure.

DRIVING

It is to the countryside that you must go, for to visit Ireland without driving through the country areas is to miss the best she has to offer. Driving is on the left-hand side of the road, which may take a little getting used to if you drive on the right at home, so avoid driving in cities until you feel comfortable with the system. If your arrival city is Dublin, do not pick your car up until you are ready to leave for the countryside. A valid driver's license from your home country is required. Your car will not be an automatic unless you specifically reserve one. Petrol (gasoline) is extremely expensive.

In the Republic, people often do not use road numbers when giving directions: they refer to roads as where they might lead to (e.g., the Cork road). To add to the confusion, new road signs quote distances in kilometers, while old signs are in miles. The Irish seem to use neither, always quoting distances in the number of hours it takes them to drive.

Introduction: About Ireland

The distances in Ireland are not great, but often the roads are not great either—though they are getting a lot better. Plan on being in a traffic jam every time a road goes through a town. Roads and motorways around Dublin are nearly always congested. Estimate your journey on the basis of an average of 30 miles (about 50 kilometers) per hour.

The types of roads found in Ireland are as follows:

MOTORWAYS: The letter "M" precedes these fast roads, which have two or three lanes of traffic either side of a central divider. Motorways are more prevalent in Northern Ireland though they are becoming more common between larger towns in the Republic.

NATIONAL ROADS: The letter "N" precedes the road number in the Republic, while in Northern Ireland, the road number is preceded by the letter "A." They are the straightest and most direct routes you can take when motorways are not available.

REGIONAL ROADS: The letter "R" precedes the road number on maps, but their numbers rarely, if ever, appear on signposts. They are usually wide enough for two cars or one tractor.

Off the major routes, road signs are not posted as often as you might wish, so when you drive it's best to plan some extra time for asking the way. Asking the way does have its advantages—you get to experience Irish directions from natives always ready to assure you that you cannot miss your destination—which gives you the opportunity of asking another friendly local the way when you do. One of the joys of meandering along less traveled country roads is rounding a bend to find that cows and sheep take precedence over cars as they saunter up the middle of the road.

DRIVING–CAR RENTAL

Readers frequently ask our advice on car rental companies. We always use Auto Europe—a car rental broker that works with the major car rental companies to find the lowest possible price. They also offer motor homes and chauffeur services. Auto Europe's toll-free phone service, from every European country, connects you to their U.S.-based, 24-hour reservation center (ask for the Europe Phone Numbers Card to be mailed to you). Auto Europe offers our readers a 5% discount (cannot be combined with any other offers or promotions) and, occasionally, free upgrades. Be sure to use the Karen Brown ID number 99006187 to receive your discount and any special offers. You can make your own reservations online via our website, *www.karenbrown.com* (select *Auto Europe* from the home page), or by phone (800-223-5555).

INFORMATION

The Irish Tourist Board (*bord failte*) and Northern Ireland Tourist Board are invaluable sources of information. Outside Ireland, they have combined their organizations under the auspices of "Tourism Ireland." They can supply you with details on all of Ireland and, on request, specific information on accommodation in homes, farmhouses, and manors; and information on festivals, fishing, and the like. The easiest way to contact them is via *www.tourismireland.com.* You can also reach them by phone as follows:

Australia: (0)2 9299 6177

Canada: (800) 223 6470

Great Britain: 0800 0397000

New Zealand: 0 9 977 2255

USA: (800) 669 9967

Introduction: About Ireland

MAPS

Each of our driving itineraries is preceded by a map showing the route, and each hotel listing is referenced to a map at the front of the book. These are an artist's renderings and, although we have tried to include as much information as possible, you will need a more detailed map to plan your travels. Our preference is for the Michelin Map of Ireland, Map 712, where the scale is 1 centimeter to 4 kilometers (i.e. 1 inch to 6.3 miles), available in our website store *www.karenbrown.com*.

PUBS

Ireland's pubs will not disappoint. Most of the 12,000 pubs, where the Irish share ideas over frothing pints of ale and porter, have a contagious spirit and charm. Stop at a pub and you'll soon be drawn into conversation. At local pubs, musicians and dancers perform for their own enjoyment, their audience being those who stop by for a drink. If this kind of entertainment appeals to you, ask someone wherever you are staying to recommend a local pub that will have live music that night.

SHOPPING

Prices of goods are fairly standard throughout Ireland, so make your purchases as you find items you like. The most popular items to buy are hand-knitted sweaters, tweeds, crystal, china, and hand-embroidered linens.

Value Added Tax (VAT) is included in the price of your purchases. There is usually a minimum purchase requirement, but it is possible for visitors from non-EU countries to get a refund of the VAT on the goods they buy in one of two ways:

1. If the goods are shipped overseas direct from the point of purchase, the store can deduct the VAT at the time of sale.

2. If you take goods with you ask the store to issue a VAT refund receipt. On departure, **before** you check in for your flight, go to the refund office at the airport. They may ask to see your purchases. You will be given a cash refund.

About Itineraries

To keep you on the right track, we have created driving itineraries covering the most interesting sightseeing. If time allows, you can link the four itineraries together and travel all around Ireland. Each itinerary explores a region's scenic beauty, history, and culture, and avoids its large cities. Along the way, we suggest alternative routes and side trips (indicated in italics). At the beginning of each itinerary, we suggest our recommended pacing to help you decide the amount of time to allocate to each region. Do not try to see all of Ireland in a week—this is frankly impossible. You will enjoy yourself much more if you concentrate on a smaller number of destinations and stay for at least a couple of nights in each, rather than spending most of your precious vacation rushing from place to place. The capricious changes in the weather mean that often what appears sparkling and romantic in sunshine, appears dull and depressing under gathering storm clouds. If the weather is stormy, find a nice place to stay with good company. Once the rain clears, there is much to see. Each itinerary is preceded by an artist's rendering of the proposed route, and outlined on the color maps at the front of the book. We suggest that you outline this on a commercial map: our preference is the Michelin Map of Ireland where the scale is 1 centimeter to 4 kilometers (1/400,000).

Introduction: About Itineraries

Overview Map: Driving Itineraries

The North

Rosgull Peninsula

Tory Island

Giant's Causeway

Glencolumbkille

Donegal

Belfast

Céide Fields

Sligo

The West

Lough Gill

Achill Island

Crossmolina

Inishbofin Island

Connemara

Dublin Walking Tour

Clifden

Dublin

Galway

Burren

Aran Islands

Kilkenny

Limerick

Cashel

Dingle Peninsula

Waterford

The Southeast

Killarney

Ring of Kerry

Kenmare

Blarney

Skellig Michael

Cork

Youghal

Kinsale

Beara Peninsula

The Southwest

Itinerary Route

Alternative Routes & Sidetrips

About Places to Stay

This book does not cover the many, modern hotels in Ireland with their look-alike bedrooms, televisions, and direct-dial phones. Rather, it offers a selection of personally recommended lodgings that cover the widest range, from a very basic, clean room in a simple farmhouse to a sumptuous suite in an elegant, castle hotel. In some, the decor is less than perfect, but the one thing they all have in common is that their owners offer wholehearted hospitality. We have inspected each and every one, and have stayed in a great many. The accommodations selected are the kind of places that we enjoy. We have tried to be candid and honest in our appraisals and to convey each listing's special flavor so that you know what to expect and will not be disappointed. To help you appreciate and understand what to expect when staying at listings in this guide, the following pointers are given in alphabetical order, not in order of importance.

CHILDREN

The majority of listings in this guide welcome children. A great many places offer family rooms with a double and one or two single beds in a room. If you want to tuck your children up in bed and enjoy a leisurely dinner, many of the listings will—with advance notice—provide an early supper for children.

CHRISTMAS

If the information section indicates that the listing is open during the Christmas holiday season, there is a very good chance that it offers a festive Christmas package.

CREDIT CARDS

Whether or not an establishment accepts credit cards is indicated in the list of icons at the bottom of each description by the symbol ▭CREDIT. We have also specified in the accommodation description which cards are accepted as follows: none, AX–American Express, MC–MasterCard, VS–Visa, or simply, all major.

DIRECTIONS

We give concise driving directions to guide you to the listing, which is often in a more out-of-the-way place than the town or village in the address. We would be very grateful if you would let us know of cases where our directions have proven inadequate.

ELECTRICITY

The voltage is 240. Most hotels, guesthouses, and farmhouses have American-style razor points for 110 volts. If you are coming from overseas, it is recommended that you take only dual-voltage appliances and a kit of electrical plugs. Your host can usually loan you a hairdryer or an iron.

HANDICAP FACILITIES

If there is *at least* one guestroom that is accessible by wheelchair, it is noted with the symbol ♿. This is not the same as saying it meets full disability standards. In reality, it can be anything from a basic ground-floor room to a fully equipped facility. Please discuss your requirements when you call your chosen place to stay to see if they have accommodation that is suitable for you.

HIDDEN IRELAND

Several of the listings are members of Hidden Ireland, a consortium of private houses that open their doors to a handful of guests at a time. All houses are of architectural merit and character with owners to match. These are the kinds of houses where you can indulge yourself by staying with people who have mile-long driveways, grand dining rooms watched over by redoubtable ancestors, four-poster beds that you have to climb into, and vast billiard rooms. The kinds of places most of us can only dream of living in, but where you are very welcome as guests because you are the ones who help the owners pay their central heating bills, school fees, and gardeners. Guests become a part of the household and family life carries on around you—you are not expected to scuttle up to your room. Everyone usually dines together round a polished table and, unless you make special requests, you eat what is served to you. The conversation flows and you meet people you might never have met elsewhere. Early or late in the season, you may find that you are the only guests and you can enjoy a romantic, candlelit dinner in a house full of character and charm. There are lakes full of salmon and stylish modern bedrooms at Delphi, gigantic old-fashioned bedrooms at Temple House, homey friendliness at Lorum Old Rectory, and delightful thematically decorated bedrooms at Quay House. When a property is a member of this group, we note it at the bottom of the description.

ICONS

We have these icons in the guidebooks and more on our website, *www.karenbrown.com.*
❄ Air conditioning in rooms, ⊥ Beach nearby, ☕ Breakfast included in room rate,
♟ Children welcome, ☕ Cooking classes offered, 🔲 Credit cards accepted,
🔥 Dinner served upon request, ☎ Direct-dial telephone in room, 🐕 Dogs by special
request, 🛗 Elevator, 🏃 Exercise room, @ Internet access available for guests,
🍸 Mini-refrigerator in rooms, ⊗ Some non-smoking rooms, P Parking available (free
or paid), 🍴 Restaurant, ♣ Spa (treatments/massage etc.), ≋ Swimming pool,
🎾 Tennis, 📺 Television with English channels in guestrooms, 💍 Wedding facilities,
♿ Wheelchair friendly, W Wireless available for guests, 🏌 Golf course nearby,
🚶 Hiking trails nearby, 🐎 Horseback riding nearby, ⛷ Skiing nearby, 🏄 Water
sports nearby, 🍷 Wineries nearby. Icons allow us to provide additional information about
our recommended properties.

When using our website to supplement the guides, positioning the cursor over an icon
will give you further details. Icons allow us to provide additional information about our
recommended properties.

IRELAND'S BLUE BOOK

Several of our listings are members of the Irish Country Houses Association, usually
referred to as The Blue Book because of the distinctive blue color of its brochure. This is
an association of owner-managed country houses, hotels, and restaurants. The majority
are country house hotels offering accommodation in charming surroundings with
restaurants, bars, and room service. However, there are several members who welcome
guests to their ancestral homes on house-party lines (much as members of Hidden
Ireland) with no bar and a set dinner menu. When a property is a member of this group,
we note it at the bottom of the description.

MAPS

At the front of the book are four regional maps showing each recommended place to stay's location. The pertinent regional map number is given at the right on the top line of each accommodation's description.

MEALS

Owners of guesthouses, farmhouses, and bed & breakfasts are often happy to serve an evening meal, if you make arrangements 24 hours in advance. Country houses offer a set menu of more elaborate fare and most offer interesting wines—again, arrangements to dine must be made 24 hours in advance. Whether or not an establishment offers dinner is indicated in the list of icons at the bottom of each description by the symbol 🌋. **You cannot just arrive and expect dinner.** Hotels and restaurants offer menus and wine lists, giving you more dining choices. If an establishment has a restaurant we indicate it with a 🍴. Our suggestion is that you make arrangements for dinner on the night of your arrival at the same time as you make reservations for accommodation.

RATES

Rates are those quoted to us, either verbally or by correspondence, for 2009. The rates given generally cover the least expensive to the most expensive double room (two people sharing a room) inclusive of taxes and, in most cases, breakfast and likewise for suites if appropriate. We do not quote rates for a single person occupying a room. When a listing does not include breakfast in its rates, we mention this in the description. We feel a great deal of resentment when an obligatory service charge of 10–15% is added to the bill, and feel that establishments often use this as a way of padding their rates. Forewarned is forearmed, so we have indicated if an establishment adds a service charge. Please **always check** prices and terms when making a reservation. Rates are quoted in euros in the Republic of Ireland and pounds sterling in Northern Ireland. Prices vary considerably and, on the whole, reflect the type of house in which you will be staying. From the charm of a simple farmhouse to the special ambiance of a vast sporting estate, each listing reflects the Irish way of life.

RESERVATIONS

When making your reservations, be sure to identify yourself as a "Karen Brown Traveler." The hotels appreciate your visit, value their inclusion in our guide, frequently tell us they take special care of our readers, and many offer special rates to Karen Brown members (visit our website at *www.karenbrown.com*). We hear over and over again that the people who use our guides are such wonderful guests!

It is important to understand that once reservations for accommodation are confirmed, whether verbally by phone or in writing, you are under contract. This means that the proprietor is obligated to provide the accommodation that was promised, and that you are obligated to pay for it. If you cannot, you are liable for a portion of the accommodation charges plus your deposit. Although some proprietors do not strictly enforce a cancellation policy many, particularly the smaller properties in our book, simply cannot afford not to do so. Similarly, many airline tickets cannot be changed or refunded without penalty. We recommend insurance to cover these types of additional expenses arising from cancellation due to unforeseen circumstances.

Reservations should always be made in advance for Dublin accommodation. In the countryside, space is not so tight and a room can often be had simply by calling in the morning. July and August are the busiest times and if you are traveling to a popular spot, you should make advance reservations. Be specific as to what your needs are, such as a ground-floor room, en suite shower, twin beds, family room. Check the prices, which may well have changed from those given in the book (2009). Ask what deposit to send or give your credit card number. Tell them about what time you intend to arrive and request dinner if you want it. There are several options for making reservations.

EMAIL: This is our preferred way of making a reservation. If the hotel/bed & breakfast is on our website and has email, its web page contains a link to its email. (Always spell out the month as the Irish reverse the American month/day numbering system.)

FAX: If you have access to a fax machine, this is a very quick way to reach a hotel/bed & breakfast. If the place to stay has a fax, we have included the number in the listing. (See EMAIL above about spelling out the month.)

LETTER: If you write for reservations, you will usually receive your confirmation and a map. You should then send your deposit. (See comment on EMAIL about spelling out month.)

TELEPHONE: By telephoning you have your answer immediately, so if space is not available, you can then decide on an alternative. If calling from the United States, allow for the time difference (Ireland is five hours ahead of New York) so that you can call during their business day. Dial 011 (the international code), 353 (Republic of Ireland's code) **or** 44 (Northern Ireland's code), then the city code (dropping the 0), and the telephone number.

SELF-CATERING ACCOMMODATION

An excellent way to explore an area is to rent self-catering accommodation on a weekly basis. You can unpack your bags, put your feet up and make yourself at home, come and go as you please, and eat what you like when you like. Tir Na Fiúise in Terryglass, and Farran House in Farran are exclusively self-catering properties. Several of the country houses that operate as bed & breakfasts can be rented in their entirety as luxurious homes. A great many listings have additional houses, cottages, and converted outbuildings that range from former coach houses to a one-time hen house. Because our primary focus is on beds, breakfasts, and evening meals, we often do not have space to discuss self-catering accommodation at length. We quote a range of rates: from the smallest unit in the low season to the largest unit in the high season, on a weekly or daily basis. Please discuss your requirements when contacting owners to see if they have accommodation that is suitable for you.

SIGHTSEEING

We have tried to mention sightseeing attractions near each lodging to encourage you to spend several nights in each location.

WEBSITE

Please visit the Karen Brown website (*www.karenbrown.com*) in conjunction with this book. Our website provides trip planning assistance, new discoveries, post-press updates, feedback from you, our readers, the opportunity to purchase goods and services that we recommend (rail tickets, car rental, travel insurance, etc.), and one-stop shopping for our guides, associated maps and watercolor prints. Most of our favorite places to stay are featured with color photos and direct website and email links. Also, we invite you to participate in the Karen Brown's Readers' Choice Awards. Be sure to visit our website and vote so your favorite properties will be honored.

Dublin Walking Tour

To Dublin Airport

Dublin Writers Museum

Parnell Square

Gate Theatre

Dublin Tourism Office

Connolly Station

GPO

Customs House

To Bullock Harbour

River Lifey

O'Connell Bridge

Four Courts

Bank of Ireland

Dublina

Christ Church

Trinity College

To Guinness Brewery

Dublin Castle

Powerscourt Townhouse

National Gallery

Merrion Square

St Patrick's Cathedral

Number 29

St. Stephen's Green

Newman House

To Bray and Wicklow

To Ballsbridge

KEY
1. The Clarence
2. The Merrion
3. Shelbourne Hotel
4. Number 31
5. Mespil Hotel
6. Waterloo House
▪▪▪▪ Walking Tour

19

Walking Tour

"In Dublin's fair city, where the girls are so pretty . . ." goes the popular old ballad. The girls are certainly pretty and the city fair, if you can overlook the rash of modern office developments begun in the 1960s and the areas that have been razed and seemingly abandoned. Dublin now appears to have seen the error of its ways and efforts are being made to restore what the bulldozers have spared. A car is more trouble than it is worth in Dublin. If your visit here is at the outset of your trip, we suggest that you not get your car until you are ready to leave or—if Dublin is a stop on your trip—park it for the duration of your stay. Dublin is a walking town, so don comfortable shoes and set out to explore the buildings, streets, and shops of this bustling, friendly city. If you feel weary along the way, there is no shortage of pubs where you can revive yourself with a refreshing drink.

Recommended Pacing: If you select a few museums that appeal to you and simply skirt the exterior of the others, this walking tour can be accomplished in a day, which means that you will need two nights' accommodation in Dublin.

Make your first stop the **Dublin Tourism Centre**, in a sturdy, granite church on Suffolk Street. Here you can book sightseeing tours; purchase ferry, train, and bus tickets; arrange lodgings; find out what is in Dublin—and enjoy a cup of coffee. Dublin is easily explored on foot, but as an introduction take one of the double-decker sightseeing buses. The tours run every ten minutes and wind a circular route through the city with a commentary on the significance of the buildings along the route. Your ticket is valid for twenty-four hours. The bus makes frequent stops so you can take the entire tour for an overview of what there is to see and then later use it as transportation between the sights, hopping on and off to visit the places that interest you.

Our walking tour begins at the southern end of O'Connell Street where **O'Connell Bridge** spans the River Liffey dividing the north from the south of Dublin. (It is also just by the city center terminus for buses: those displaying "*An Lar*," meaning city center, usually end up here.) Turn south into **Westmoreland Street** past the somber, windowless **Bank of Ireland**, which began life in 1729 as the seat of the Irish parliament. Cross the street and enter through the front arch of **Trinity College** into the cobbled square. Founded in 1591 by Elizabeth I, it contains a fine collection of buildings from the 18th to the 20th centuries. Cross the square to the library, where a display center houses the jewel of Trinity College, the ***Book of Kells****,* a Latin text of the Four Gospels. A page of this magnificent, illuminated manuscript is turned every month and if you are not overly impressed by the page on display, return to the library bookshop and browse through a reproduction. While at the college visit **The Dublin Experience**, a sophisticated audio-visual presentation that orients you to the main events of Irish history.

Retrace your steps to the front gate and turn south into pedestrians-only **Grafton Street**, teeming with people and enlivened by street musicians. Its large, department store, **Brown Thomas**, is popular with visitors.

At the end of Grafton Street, dodge the hurrying buses and cross into the peaceful tranquility of **St. Stephen's Green**, an island of flowers, trees, and grass surrounding small lakes dotted with ducks. On the far side of the square, at 85 and 86 St. Stephen's Green, is **Newman House**, once the home of the old Catholic University (later University College Dublin), which boasted James Joyce amongst its distinguished graduates. Number 85 is restored to its pristine, aristocratic years of the 1740s. On the ground floor are wall reliefs of the god Apollo and his nine muses, done elaborately in stucco. A staircase of Cuban mahogany leads to a reception room with more riotous plasterwork figures on the ceiling. Number 86 has some rooms with interesting associations with the Whaley family and Gerard Manley Hopkins, and the Bishop's Room has been restored to its Victorian splendor.

Return to the north side of the square to the landmark **Shelbourne Hotel**, long recommended as the perfect place to enjoy afternoon tea. Follow **Merrion Row** and turn left into **Merrion Street** passing the back of **Leinster House**, the Irish Parliament. It consists of two chambers—the *Dáil*, the lower house, and the *Seanad*, the upper house or senate. You can tour the building when parliament is not in session. Adjacent to the parliament building is the **National Gallery of Ireland**, which is a Victorian building with about 3,000 works of art. There's a major collection of Ireland's greatest painter, Jack Yeats, and works by Canaletto, Goya, Titian, El Greco, Poussin, Manet, Picasso, and many others.

Merrion Square is one of Dublin's finest remaining Georgian squares and the onetime home of several famous personages—William Butler Yeats lived at 82 and earlier at 52, Daniel O'Connell at 51, and Oscar Wilde's parents occupied number 1. The jewel of Merrion Square is **Number 29** Lower Fitzwilliam Street (corner of Lower Fitzwilliam Street and Upper Mount Street), a magnificently restored, late 18th-century townhouse. From the basement through living rooms to the nursery and playroom, the house is meticulously furnished in the style of the period 1790–1820.

Stroll into **Clare Street**, stopping to browse in **Greene's Bookstore** with its lovely, old façade and tables of books outside.

Detour into **Kildare Street**, where you find the **National Museum** displaying all the finest treasures of the country. There are marvelous examples of gold, bronze, and other ornaments, as well as relics of the Viking occupation of Dublin—the 8th-century Tara Brooch is perhaps the best-known item here.

Merrion Square

Follow the railings of Trinity College to the **Kilkenny Design Centre** and **Blarney Woolen Mills**, fine places to shop for Irish crafts and clothing.

With your back to the front gate of Trinity College, cross into **Dame Street**, where the statue of Henry Grattan, a famous orator, stands with arms outstretched outside the parliament building. Walk along Dame Street past Dublin's most famous 1960s "modern" building, the **Central Bank**, which looks like egg boxes on stilts. Go under the bank and you are in **Temple Bar**, with its narrow cobbled streets and little old buildings. In the daytime it's a place of coffee houses and little shops. At night its narrow streets become very vibrant as the clubs open with many good pubs and lots of restaurants—a favorite place for young people. Returning to Dame Street and a more sedate side of Dublin, you come to **Dublin Castle**, built in the early 13th century on the site of an earlier Danish fortification. The adjoining 18th-century **State Apartments** with their ornate furnishings are more impressive inside than out.

Returning to Dame Street, you pass **City Hall** and, on your right, the impressive **Christ Church Cathedral** comes into view. Dedicated in 1192, it has been rebuilt and restored many times. After the Reformation when the Protestant religion was imposed on the Irish people, it became a Protestant cathedral (Church of Ireland). The large crypt remained as a gathering spot and marketplace for the locals (Catholics) who used it for many years, until a rector expelled them because their rowdiness was interrupting church services. Another point of interest is **Strongbow's Tomb**: he was one of the most famous Norman lords of Ireland and, by tradition, debts were paid across his tomb. When a wall collapsed and crushed it, a replacement—an unknown crusader's tomb—was conscripted and named Strongbow's Tomb.

Joined to the cathedral by a covered bridge arching across the street is **Dublina**, where you learn the history of Dublin through an audio-visual display. You conclude your tour at the large-scale model of the city and the gift shop.

At the junction of High Street and Bridge Street, pause to climb the restored remains of a portion of **Dublin's Walls**. When they were built in 1240, the walls fronted onto the River Liffey.

Just down **Thomas Street** is that thriving Dublin institution, the **Guinness Brewery**, whence flows the national drink. As you near your goal, the smell of roasting grains permeates the air. The Guinness Storehouse, a 7-story glass atrium, is built on the site where Arthur Guinness first signed his 9000-year brewery lease in 1759. Journey through the history of the brewing process, learn the story of the Guinness family, and end your tour with a pint of the black stuff in the Gravity bar with its panoramic views of the city. Of course there are lots of opportunities to purchase souvenirs of all-things Guinness.

If you decide not to visit the Guinness Brewery, cross diagonally from the walls to the **Brazen Head** in **Bridge Street**, where you can enjoy that same brew in Dublin's oldest pub. There has been a tavern on this site since Viking times, though the present, rather dilapidated, premises date from 1688. It's always a crowded spot that comes alive late in the evening, when musicians gather for impromptu sessions of traditional music.

Cross the River Liffey and, strolling along the **Inns Quay**, you come to the **Four Courts**, the supreme and high courts of Ireland. You can look inside the fine, circular waiting hall under the beautiful green dome, which allows light through its apex.

Turn left up **Capel Street** and make the third right into **Mary Street** which leads to the busiest pedestrian shopping street in Dublin, **Henry Street**. A short detour down **Moore Street** takes you through Dublin's colorful open-air fruit, vegetable, and flower market.

On reaching **O'Connell Street**, turn left. O'Connell Street has its share of tourist traps and hamburger stores, but it's a lively bunch of Dubliners who walk its promenades—placard-carrying nuns, nurses collecting for charity, hawkers of fruit, flowers, and plastic trinkets—all are there for you to see as you stroll along this wide boulevard and continue past the **Gate Theatre** into **Parnell Square**. At the north end of the square in a restored 18th-century mansion, you find the **Dublin Writers Museum**, where you can view the paintings and memorabilia with an audio tape telling you all about them. Among those featured are George Bernard Shaw, William Butler Yeats, Oscar Wilde, James Joyce, and Samuel Beckett.

Retrace your steps down O'Connell Street to the **General Post Office**. The GPO, as it is affectionately known, is a national shrine known as the headquarters of the 1916 revolution. Pass the statue of Daniel O'Connell and the millennium "spike" and you are back at your starting point, O'Connell Bridge.

Four Courts

The Southeast

- ● Orientation/ Sightseeing
- ▬ ▬ Itinerary Route
- ▬ Roads
- ▪ ▪ ▪ Alternative Route & Sidetrips
- ✈ Airport

Dublin   Howth

Powerscourt Gardens & Waterfall

N11

Sally Gap

Rathnew

Glendalough   Annamoe   Wicklow

Vale of Avoca   Avoca

N9

Arklow

Gorey

R693   Kilkenny

N11

Freshford

Ferns

Cashel   N8

Enniscorthy

Cahir   N24

New Ross

Waterford   Wexford

John F. Kennedy Park

The Vee   Lismore   Passage East   Arthurstown

N25

N72   Dungarven   Tramore

N25

Youghal

Cork   N25

Belfast

Dublin

The Southeast

All too often visitors rush from Dublin through Waterford and on to western Ireland, never realizing that they are missing some of the most ancient antiquities and lovely scenery along the seductive little byways that traverse the moorlands and wind through wooded glens. This itinerary travels from Dublin into the Wicklow Mountains, pausing to admire the lovely Powerscourt Gardens, lingering amongst the ancient monastic ruins of Glendalough, visiting the Avoca handweavers who capture the subtle hues of heather and field in their fabric, and admiring the skill of the Waterford crystal cutters.

Glendalough

Recommended Pacing: If you are not a leisurely sightseer, and leave Dublin early, you can follow this itinerary and be in Youghal by nightfall. But resist the temptation—select a base for two nights in two places and explore at leisure. If you are not continuing westward and returning to Dublin via The Vee, Cashel, and Kilkenny, select a place to stay near Cashel or Kilkenny.

Leave Dublin following the N11 in the direction of Wexford. (If you have difficulty finding the correct road, follow signs for the ferry at Dun Laoghaire and, from there, pick up signs for Wexford.) As soon as the city suburbs are behind you, the road becomes a dual carriageway. Watch for signs indicating an exit signposted **Enniskerry** and **Powerscourt Gardens**. Follow the winding, wooded lane to Enniskerry and bear left in the center of the village. This brings you to the main gates of Powerscourt Gardens. As you drive through the vast, parklike grounds, the mountains of Wicklow appear before you, decked in every shade of green. Powerscourt House was burnt to a ruin in 1974: a rook's nest blocked one of the chimneys, and when a fire was lit in the fireplace, the resultant blaze quickly engulfed this grand home. Restoration is under way and, while there are no grand rooms to visit, you can enjoy refreshments at the restaurant and shopping at the Avoca knitwear store. The gardens descend in grand tiers from the ruined house, as if descending into a bowl—a mirror-like lake sits at the bottom. Masses of roses adorn the walled garden and velvet, green, grassy walks lead through the woodlands. Many visitors are intrigued by the animal cemetery with its little headstones and inscriptions—not an uncommon sight in Irish stately homes. Leaving the car park, turn left for the 6-kilometer drive to the foot of **Powerscourt Waterfall**, the highest waterfall in Ireland and a favorite summer picnic place for many Dubliners.

Turn to the left as you leave the waterfall grounds to meander along narrow country lanes towards **Glencree**. As you come upon open moorland, take the first turn left for the 8-kilometer uphill drive to the summit of **Sally Gap**. This road is known as the "old military road" because it follows the path that the British built across these wild mountains to aid them in their attempts to suppress the feisty men of County Wicklow.

Powerscourt Gardens

Neat stacks of turf are piled to dry in the sun. Grazing sheep seem to be the only occupants of this vast, rolling moorland. Below **Glenmacnass Waterfall**, the valley opens up to a patchwork of fields beckoning you to **Laragh** and Glendalough.

Glendalough, a monastic settlement of seven churches, was founded by St. Kevin in the 6th century. After St. Patrick, St. Kevin is Ireland's most popular saint. He certainly picked a stunning site in this wooded valley between two lakes to found his monastic order. Amidst the tilting stones of the graveyard, the round tower—still perfect after more than a thousand years—punctuates the skyline. The Interpretive Centre presents a 15-minute movie and display on the history of the area. Take time to follow the track beyond Glendalough to the Upper Lake (you can also drive there). Tradition has it that St. Kevin lived a solitary life in a hut near here. Farther up on a cliff face is a cave known as St.

Kevin's Bed. Here, so the story goes, Kathleen—a beautiful temptress—tried to seduce the saint who, to cool her advances, threw her into the lake.

Retrace the road to Laragh, turn right, and travel south through the village of Rathdrum where sturdy stone cottages line the street, and continue through the crossroad following signposts for **Avondale House**, the home of Charles Stewart Parnell. Parnell was born into the ruling Anglo-Irish gentry; but, due in part to the influence of his more open-minded mother, an American, he became the leading light in Ireland's political fight for independence. His downfall was his long-term affair with a married English lady. The house is sparsely furnished and takes just a few minutes to tour. You can also wander around the estate with its wonderful trees.

Leave Avondale to the left and you soon join the main road that takes you through the **Vale of Avoca** to the "Meeting of the Waters" at the confluence of the rivers Avonmore and Avonbeg. Detour into **Avoca** to visit the **Avoca Handweavers**. You are welcome to wander amongst the skeins and bobbins of brightly hued wool to see the weavers at work and talk to them above the noise of the looms. An adjacent shop sells tweeds and woolens.

At **Arklow** join the N11, a broad, fast road taking you south through Gorey and Ferns to **Enniscorthy**. Amidst the gray stone houses, built on steeply sloping ground by the River Slaney, lies a Norman castle. Rebuilt in 1586, the castle houses a folk museum that includes exhibits from the Stone Age to the present day, with emphasis on the part played by local people in the 1798 rebellion against English rule.

Take the N30 towards Waterford and just before **New Ross**, turn left towards Arthurstown. After about 1 kilometer, turn right for the **Kennedy Homestead** in **Dunganstown**, where the great-grandfather of American President John F. Kennedy lived before being driven from Ireland by the terrible potato famine of the 1840s. His simple, family cottage has been rather overly restored, but the rural location has changed little since the American branch of the family left Ireland. Interestingly, the farm is still owned by a Kennedy. (*Tel: 051 388264, email info@kennedyhomestead.com.*) Leaving the homestead, continue along the country lane to the main road and the **John F. Kennedy Arboretum**, a memorial to the slain president of row upon row of trees.

Leave the arboretum towards Arthurstown and, at the first Y in the road, take the right-hand fork for the short drive to Great Island and **Kilmokea** at **Campile** with its 7 acres of lovely gardens. Around the house are the formal, walled gardens and a heavy, wooden door set into the stone wall leading you to the winding paths of the woodland garden. Enjoy an excellent lunch or afternoon tea in the conservatory tearoom, and ask for directions for the short cut down narrow lanes to **Arthurstown**, where the **Passage East ferry** takes you across the estuary to **Passage East**, the tiny village on the western shores of Waterford harbor. Arriving at the N25, you turn right to visit the town of **Waterford** fronting the River Suir, and left to arrive at the **Waterford Crystal Factory**. This is a very worthwhile excursion, as the tours give you an appreciation for why these hand-blown, hand-cut items are so expensive. It takes many years to become a master craftsman, and one little mistake in the intricate cutting means painstaking hours of work are wasted and the defective item is simply smashed and recycled—there are no seconds. (Waterford crystal items are uniformly priced throughout the country.) It is a very popular venue, the stopping place for seemingly every coach tour. Fortunately, separate transportation is provided to shuttle individual tourists to and from the factory. I thoroughly enjoyed touring with a guide who allowed plenty of time to watch the skilled workmen. The showroom displays the full line of Waterford's production, from shimmering chandeliers to sparkling stemware. The visitors' center also has a gift shop, tourist information center, and café.

If the weather is inclement, stay on the N25 in the direction of Cork, but otherwise meander along the coast road by doubling back in the direction of Waterford for a **very short** distance, turning to the right to **Tramore**, a family holiday town, long a favorite of the "ice-cream-and-bucket-and-spade" brigade. Skirting the town, follow the beautiful coastal road through **Annestown** to **Dungarvan**.

Where the coastal road meets the N25, detour from your route, turning sharp left to **Shell House**. Like it or hate it, there is nothing quite like it on any suburban street in the world—a cottage where all available wall surfaces are decorated with colored shells in various patterns.

Returning to the main road after crossing Dungarvan harbor, the N25 winds up and away from the coast, presenting lovely views of the town and the coast. If you haven't eaten, try **Seanachie** (a restored, thatched farmhouse, now a traditional restaurant and bar), which sits atop the hill and serves good Irish and Continental food. After passing through several kilometers of forests, turn left on the R673 to **Ardmore**, following the coastline to the village. Beyond the neatly painted houses clustered together lies the **Ardmore Monastic Site**. The well-preserved round tower used to have six internal timber landings joined by ladders, and at the top was a bell to call the monks to prayer or warn of a hostile raid. The round tower is unique to Ireland, its entrance door placed well above the ground: entry was gained by means of a ladder, which could be drawn up whenever necessary. Early Christian monks built round towers as protection against Vikings and other raiders. Leaving the ruins, turn left in the village for **Youghal** where this itinerary ends. Sightseeing in Youghal is outlined in the following itinerary. From Youghal you can continue west to follow *The Southwest* itinerary, or take the following alternative route back to Dublin via The Vee, Cashel, and Kilkenny.

Youghal

ROUTE FROM YOUGHAL TO DUBLIN VIA THE VEE, CASHEL, AND KILKENNY

From Youghal, retrace your steps towards Waterford to the bridge that crosses the River Blackwater, and turn sharp left (before you cross the river) on **Blackwater Valley Drive**, a narrow road which follows the broad, muddy waters of the Blackwater through scenic wooded countryside. The "drive" is well-signposted as "Scenic Route." Quiet country roads bring you into **Lismore**. Turn left into town and right at the town square. Cross the river and take the second road to the left, following signs for **Clogheen** and **The Vee**. As the road climbs, woods give way to heathery moorlands climbing to the summit where the valley opens before you—a broad "V" shape framing an endless patchwork of fields in every shade of green.

Rock of Cashel

The Southeast

Continue on to **Cahir Castle**, which has stood on guard to defend the surrounding town of **Cahir** since 1375. A guided tour explains the elaborate defensive system, making a visit here both interesting and informative. A separate audio-visual presentation provides information about the castle and other monuments in the area.

Leaving the castle, continue through the town square for the 16-kilometer drive to **Cashel**. The **Rock of Cashel** seems to grow out of the landscape as you near the town and you can see why this easily defensible site was the capital for the kings of Munster as long ago as 370 A.D. In the course of converting Ireland to Christianity, St. Patrick reached the castle and, according to legend, jabbed his staff into the king's foot during the conversion ceremony. The king apparently took it all very stoically, thinking it was part of the ritual. Upon reaching the summit of the rock, you find a 10th-century round tower, a 13th-century cathedral, and a 15th-century entrance building or Hall of Vicars Choral—a building which was sensitively restored in the 1970s and now houses some exhibits including St. Patrick's Cross, an ancient Irish high cross of unusual design. If you overnight in or near Cashel, be sure to enjoy **Brú Ború**, a foot-tapping evening of traditional Irish entertainment in the theater below the Rock.

Leave Cashel on the N8 for the 40-kilometer drive northeast to **Urlingford**, where you bear right through **Freshford** for the 27-kilometer drive to **Kilkenny** (see listings). Kilkenny is quite the loveliest of Irish towns and it is easy to spend a day here sightseeing and shopping. Entering the town, turn left at the first traffic lights along the main street and park your car outside the castle.

Kilkenny Castle was originally built between 1195 and 1207. The imposing building, as it now stands, is a mixture of Tudor and Gothic design and is definitely worth a visit. The east wing picture gallery is flooded by natural light from the skylights in the roof and displays a collection of portraits of the Ormonde family, the owners of Kilkenny Castle from 1391 until 1967.

Opposite the castle entrance, the stables now house the **Kilkenny Design Centre**, a retail outlet for goods of Irish design and production: silver jewelry, knits, textiles, furniture, and crafts.

Undoubtedly, the best way to see the medieval buildings of Kilkenny is on foot. A walking tour starts from the tourist office in the **Shee Alms House**, just a short distance from the castle. Stroll up High Street into Parliament Street to **Rothe House**. The house, built in 1594 as the home of Elizabethan merchant John Rothe, is now a museum depicting how such a merchant lived. You should also see **St. Canice's Cathedral** at the top of Parliament Street. The round tower dates from the 6th century, when St. Canice founded a monastic order here. Building began on the cathedral in 1251, though most of the lovely church you see today is an 1864 restoration.

Alleyways, with fanciful names such as The Butter Slip, lead you from the High Street to St. Kieran Street where you find **Kylters Inn**, the oldest building in town. This historic inn has a lurid history—supposedly a hostess of many centuries ago murdered four successive husbands, was then accused of witchcraft, and narrowly escaped being burnt at the stake by fleeing to the Continent.

This is an area noted for its craftspeople (leatherworkers, potters, painters) and culinary artists, resulting in a plethora of restaurants and craft shops in the surrounding villages, making this a very interesting area in which to spend several days. I always head for the **Nicholas Mosse Pottery** in Bennetsbridge where you can purchase quality seconds, as well as watch skilled potters making and decorating this classic spongewear.

The Southwest

Legend:
- ● Orientation/Sightseeing
- – – Itinerary Route
- —— Roads
- ▪▪▪▪ Alternative Route & Sidetrips
- ✈ Airport

See inset map

Shannon Airport
Limerick
Tarbert
Adare
N20
N21
Belfast
Dublin
Ballydavid
Tralee
N21
Dingle Peninsula
Castleisland
N22
N23
Dingle
Killorglin
Killarney
Mallow
N70
Gap of Dunloe
Cahersiveen
Ring of Kerry
N71
Portmagee
Sneem
Kenmare
N22
Blarney
Midleton
Waterville
Cork
Skellig Michael
Caherdaniel
Glengarriff
Youghal
Beara Peninsula
Ballylickey
Kinsale
Bantry
Cobh
N71
Clonakilty
N71

The Southwest

The scenery of the southwest is absolutely magnificent: the mellow charm of Kinsale Harbor, the rugged landscape that winds you towards Glengarriff and its island filled with subtropical vegetation, the pretty 19th-century town of Kenmare, the translucent lakes of Killarney, and the ever-changing light on spectacular seascapes on the Dingle Peninsula. Relish the fabled beauties of this lovely part of Ireland. Take time to detour to Blarney to take part in the tradition of climbing atop Blarney Castle to kiss the stone that is said to confer "the gift of the gab." Do not hurry: allow time to linger over breakfast, enjoy a chat over a glass of Guinness, sample fresh salmon and scallops, and join in an evening singsong in a local pub.

Kinsale

Recommended Pacing: For this itinerary, select two places to stay near the coast, one in either Kenmare or Killarney, and one in Dingle. Allow one or two nights in each spot.

Your journey to the southwest begins in **Youghal** (pronounced "yawl"). Sir Walter Raleigh, who introduced the potato and tobacco from the New World, was once its mayor. It's a pleasant, old town dominated by the clock tower, which was built in 1776 and served as the town's jail. The one-way traffic system makes it impossible to explore without parking the car and walking. Several of the Main Street shops have been refurbished, but the town still has an unspoiled look to it. Make your first stop the **Heritage Centre** with its displays on the town, where you can pick up a brochure that outlines a walking tour of the old buildings.

Traveling the N25, a 30-kilometer drive brings you to the heart of **Midleton** where you find the **Jameson Heritage Centre** in the old whiskey distillery. Marvel at the world's largest pot distillery in the courtyard (capacity 143,872 liters), learn about whiskey production, visit the huge waterwheel, and be rewarded by a sample of the golden liquor. There's also a shop and café.

Nearby **Cobh** (pronounced "cove") was renamed Queenstown to mark the visit of Queen Victoria in 1849 and reverted back to Cobh in 1922. There's a long tradition of naval operations here, as its large harbor is a safe anchorage. The **Cobh Experience**, an audio-visual display housed in the restored Victorian railway station, tells the story of this port. Cobh was the point of departure for many emigrants off to seek a better life in America and Australia. For many it was the last piece of Irish soil they stood on before taking a boat to a new life. The ill-fated *Lusitania* was torpedoed not far from Cobh and survivors were brought here. It was also the last port of call of the *Titanic*. There's an excellent shop and café—an enjoyable place to spend a couple of hours on a rainy day.

Retrace your steps a short distance to the **Carriagaloe-Glenbrook ferry**, which transports you across Cork harbor and eliminates the hassle of driving through Cork city. A short, countryside drive brings you to **Kinsale**, its harbor full of tall-masted boats. Narrow, winding streets are lined with quaint and several sadly derelict houses lead up from the harbor. Kinsale has some attractive shops and a great variety of restaurants. For lunch, Fishy Fishy is an excellent choice. At all but the ethnic restaurants, reservations are needed for dinner. It's a pleasant pastime to check the menus on display as you inhale mouth-watering aromas and peek at happy people enjoying their food. A good way to orient yourself is to take the walking tour which leaves the tourist office at 11:15 am.

There has been a fortress in Kinsale since Norman times. A great battle nearby in 1601 precipitated the flight of the earls and sounded the death knell of the ancient Gaelic civilization. It was from Kinsale that James II left for exile after his defeat at Boyne Water.

About 3 kilometers east of Kinsale, the impressive, 17th-century **Charles Fort** stands guard over the entrance to its harbor. It takes several hours to tour the five bastions that make up the complex. The ordnance sheds are restored and hold a photographic and historical exhibition about the fort.

Across the estuary, you see the 1603 **James Fort** where William Penn's father was governor of Kinsale, while William worked as a clerk of the Admiralty Court. Later, William was given a land grant in America on which he founded the state of Pennsylvania.

SIDE TRIP TO BLARNEY

*About a half-hour drive north of Kinsale lie **Blarney Castle** and its famous tourist attraction, the **Blarney Stone**. Kissing the Blarney Stone, by climbing atop the keep and hanging upside-down, is said to confer the "gift of the gab." Even if you are not inclined to join in this backbreaking, unhygienic pursuit, the castle is worth a visit. The gardens are beautiful, there's several well-signposted walks, the village is adorable with its shops round the village green, and there's a great shopping opportunity at **Blarney Woolen Mills** for all things Irish, particularly knitwear.*

Blarney Castle

Leave Kinsale along the harbor, cross the River Bandon, and follow country lanes to the sleepy, little village of **Ballinspittle**. As you drive through the village, it is hard to imagine that in 1985 it was overwhelmed by pilgrims. They came to the village shrine after a local girl reported seeing the statue of the Virgin Mary rocking back and forth. You pass the shrine on your right just before you come to the village. Follow country lanes to **Timoleague**, a very small coastal village watched over by the ruins of a Franciscan abbey, and on to the N71 and **Clonakilty** and **Skibbereen**. As you travel westwards, rolling fields in every shade of green present themselves.

Arriving at the waterfront in **Bantry**, you come to **Bantry House**. Like so many other Irish country houses, it has seen better days, but the present owner, Egerton Shelswell-White, makes visitors welcome and gives a typed information sheet—in the language of your choice—that guides you room-by-room through the house. The house has a wonderful collection of pictures, furniture, and works of art, brought together by the second Earl of Bantry during his European travels in the first half of the 19th century. In contrast to his ancestors' staid portraits, Egerton is shown playing his trombone.

Apart from furnishing the house, the second Earl, inspired by the gardens of Europe, laid out a formal Italian garden and a "staircase to the sky," the steep terraces rising up to the crest of the hill behind the house. There's a marvelous view of the house and Bantry Bay from the top. If you are not up to the climb, you can still enjoy a magnificent, though less lofty view across the boat-filled bay from the terrace in front of the house. A very pleasant cafe occupies the old kitchen. One wing of the house has been renovated and modernized to provide upmarket bed & breakfast accommodation.

In the stable block next to the house, the **1796 Bantry French Armada Centre** relates the story of the French Armada's attempt to invade Ireland in 1796. It failed and a model of one of the armada's ships that sank in Bantry Bay is on display—a very interesting look at a little-known piece of Irish history.

Eight kilometers north lies **Ballylickey**.

SIDE TRIP TO GOUGANE BARRA LAKE

*From Ballylickey an inland excursion takes you to **Gougane Barra Lake**, a beautiful lake locked into a ring of mountains. Here you find a small hotel where you can stop for a snack or a warming drink, and a little church on an island in the lake, the oratory where St. Finbarr went to contemplate and pray. The road to and from the lake takes you over a high pass and through mountain tunnels.*

Continue along the N71 and just before you enter **Glengarriff**, turn left for the harbor to take a ferryboat for the ten-minute ride to Garinish Island, a most worthwhile trip. (*Harbour Queen Ferryboats, tel: 027 63116, fax: 027 63298.*) **Garinish Island**, once a barren rock where only gorse and heather grew, was transformed into a miniature botanical paradise at the beginning of this century by a Scottish politician, Arran Bryce. The sheltered site of the island provides perfect growing conditions for trees, shrubs, and flowers from all over the world. It took a hundred men over three years to sculpt this lovely spot with its formal Italian garden, caseta, and temple.

From Glengarriff, the road winds upwards and, glancing behind, you have a spectacular view of **Bantry Bay** lying beyond a patchwork of green fields. Rounding the summit, the road tunnels through a large buttress of rock and you emerge to stunning views of sparse, rocky hillsides.

Cross the River Kenmare into **Kenmare**. This delightful town of gray stone houses, with gaily painted shopfronts lining two broad main streets, is a favorite with tourists who prefer its peace and charm to the hectic pace of Killarney. Kenmare is full of excellent shops: **Cleo's** has outstanding knitwear, **Quills** has vast quantities of woolens, **Brenmar Jon** sells top-of-the-line fine knitwear, **The Craft Shop** offers souvenirs and pottery, and **Nostalgia** offers antique and new linen and lace. The town also has some delightful restaurants: **The Purple Heather**, a daytime bistro; **Packies**, a lively restaurant; the charming **Lime Tree** restaurant in the Old Schoolhouse; and **The Park Hotel** with its opulent afternoon silver-service teas and superb restaurant. Visit the **Heritage Centre** with its displays of locally made lace. Just a short walk from the Heritage Centre, the **Kenmare Stone Circle** is the largest in the southwest of Ireland. Walks abound, from strolling along the broad river estuary to strenuous hill hikes. Kenmare is a perfect base for exploring both the Iveragh (Ring of Kerry) and Beara peninsulas and for visiting Killarney. It also serves as a stepping-off point for a side trip to Skellig Michael.

SIDE TRIP TO THE BEARA PENINSULA

If you do not stop along the way, it will take you between two and three hours to drive the ***Beara Peninsula****, where the scenery is wild, but gorgeous. From Kenmare, a minor road (R571) takes you along the north shore of the peninsula to* ***Ardgroom****, a picturesque village nestled beside a little harbor at the foot of the mountains. Farther west,* ***Eyeries*** *village looks out over the Skellig Rocks and several rocky inlets. Behind the village, the mountain road rises up through the Pass of Boffickle for a fantastic view back over the bay. In the 19th century,* ***Allihies*** *was a center of the copper mining industry, but now it* *is a resort with a magnificent beach curving along the bay. At the most westerly point of the peninsula lies **Garinish**, where a cable car takes visitors over to **Dursey Island**.*

Dursey is a long, mountain island encircled by high cliffs. Offshore are several other islands, the most interesting of which is Bull Rock, a roosting place for gannets. A cave passes right through it, creating a massive rock arch.

*Skirting the southern shore of the peninsula, the narrow road hugs the ocean through **Castletownbere** and **Adrigole**, from where you can follow the coastal road into Glengarriff or take the opportunity for a spectacular view by turning left and ascending the **Healy Pass**. It's hard to turn and admire the vista of **Bantry Bay** as the road gently zigzags up the pass, so stop at the top to relish the view before continuing down to **Lauraugh,** where you turn right for Kenmare.*

SIDE TRIP TO IVERAGH PENINSULA—RING OF KERRY

Instead of following our itinerary, you can use the Ring of Kerry as a route to Dingle or Killarney, or as a daytrip, traveling this modified version of the "Ring" for a roundtrip from Kenmare to Kenmare.

While part of the drive contains some of the most magnificent scenery in Ireland (between Kenmare and Waterville), some of it is not particularly inspiring (the northern stretch from Waterville to Killorglin) so we recommend that you leave the "Ring" in Waterville and travel cross country to Glencar—thereby avoiding the boring bit. Hope that the fickle Irish weather is at its best for when mists wreathe the scenery, it takes a lot of imagination to conjure up inspiring views as you drive down fog-shrouded lanes. Even if the weather is dull, don't lose heart, at any moment the sun could break through. Traffic is heavier on the Ring during the summer months when there are more cars and coaches which drive around the Ring in an anti-clockwise direction, starting from Killarney.

*Starting at Kenmare, a lovely drive takes you along the Kenmare river estuary with tempting glimpses of water and the Beara Peninsula. Arriving at **Sneem**, enjoy this most picturesque village with its tiny, gaily painted houses bordering two village greens.*

Continuing your journey westward you come to **Caherdaniel** village where you turn left for **Derrynane House**, the home of Daniel O'Connell, "The Liberator," a title he earned for his part in winning Catholic emancipation. If the weather is inclement, concentrate on the house with its furnished rooms, audio-visual presentation, museum, and tearooms. If the weather is fine, spend your time outdoors walking along the sandy beach of **Derrynane Bay** and crossing the narrow strip of sand that separates the mainland from **Abbey Island** where St. Fionan founded a monastic order over 1,000 years ago.

Just round the point lies **Iskeroon** (see listing in Caherdaniel) and **Bunavalla** pier where boats leave for the Skellig Islands (see "Side Trip to Skellig Michael"). A panoramic view of Derrynane Bay can be enjoyed from the **Scariff Inn**—you cannot miss this landmark, a bright-red pub sitting beside the road 3 kilometers above the seashore.

Cresting the **Coomakista Pass**, drive to **Waterville**, an aptly named town surrounded by the ocean on one side and lakes on the other. From here leave the traditional Ring and instead of going to Killarney via Cahersiveen follow a much quieter and more scenic route via Glencar. Travel along the **Inny Valley**, through the **Ballaghisheen Forest** and over the **Ballaghisheen Pass** to **Glencar**. From Glencar proceed to **Killorglin** and then to **Killarney** and back to **Kenmare** (see Kenmare to Killarney drive on page 48).

However, our suggested route for your return to Kenmare is to take a right-hand turn to **Caragh Lake** (5 kilometers before your reach Killorglin) and follow the narrow lanes around this beautiful lake and across the rugged **Macgillycuddy's Reeks** (Ireland's highest mountains) to Blackwater Bridge (on the Ring) and Kenmare—a trip to be undertaken only on a clear day.

SIDE TRIP TO SKELLIG MICHAEL

Skellig Michael *is a very special place, a rocky island topped by the ruins of an ancient monastery lying 12 kilometers off the coast of the Ring of Kerry. Boats run daily between Easter and October, and you need to call at least two days in advance to make a reservation. However, the trip to the island cannot be counted upon until the actual day because it depends on calm seas. Boat service operates from several harbors on the Ring of Kerry—Bunavalla: Kenneth Roddy, www.skelligtrips.com, email: ken@skelligtrips.com; Seamus Shea, tel: 066 9475129; Portmagee: Des Lavelle, tel: 066 9476124, email: lavelles@indigo.ie; or Brendan O'Keefe, Fisherman's Bar, tel: 066 9477103. Remember to wear flat-heeled shoes and take a waterproof jacket, an extra sweater, and lunch. The morning departure for the island and the late afternoon return necessitate your spending two nights on the Ring of Kerry (see listings in Caherdaniel, and Kenmare).*

After you arrive at the cove beneath the looming rock, the first part of your ascent follows the path to the abandoned lighthouse, past seabirds' nests clinging to tiny crevasses in the steep rock slopes. As you round a corner, the monks' stairway appears and you climb up hundreds and hundreds of hand-hewn stone steps to the monastery perched on a ledge, high above the pounding ocean. Pausing to catch your breath, you marvel at the monks who set out in fragile, little boats to establish this monastery and toiled with crude implements to build these steps up the sheer rock face.

At the summit, six little beehive huts, a slightly larger stone oratory, and the roofless walls of a small church nestle against the hillside, some poised at the edge—only a low stone wall between them and the churning ocean far below. The windowless interiors of the huts hardly seem large enough for a person to lie down. Remarkably, the monks' only water source was rainwater runoff stored in rock fissures. The Office of Public Works is maintaining and restoring the site and there might be someone there to impart information.

It is reputed that the monks arrived in 600 A.D. According to annals, the Vikings raided in 812 and 823 and found an established community. It is documented that the last monks departed in the 13th century. When it is time to leave this spot, you feel a sense of wonder for the men who toiled in this rocky place, enduring deprivation, hardship, and solitude to achieve a state of grace.

As a complement (or alternative) to visiting Skellig Michael, visit the **Skellig Heritage Centre** on Valencia Island. The center is found where the road bridge meets the island, directly opposite Portmagee. An audio-visual presentation, "The Call of the Skelligs," takes you to the Skellig Michael monastery while displays show the bird and sea life of the islands.

View to Little Skellig from Skellig Michael

From Kenmare travel over one of Ireland's most beautiful roads (N71) for the twisty 34-kilometer drive over mountains to Killarney, stopping at **Ladies' View** to admire a spectacular panorama with the lakes of Killarney spread at your feet.

In amongst the woodlands you find the car park for **Torc Waterfall**. Following the stream, a short uphill walk brings you to the celebrated 20-meter cascade of water.

Muckross House and Gardens are 5 kilometers out of Killarney on the Kenmare road. (Be sure to choose the entrance gate that enables you to take your car to the car park beside the house). Tudor-style Muckross was built in 1843 in an enviable position beside the lake. The main rooms are furnished in splendid Victorian style and the remainder of the house serves as a folk museum with various exhibits. There's also a bustling gift shop and tearoom. The gardens surrounding the house are lovely, containing many subtropical plants, and there is no more delightful way to tour the grounds than by horse and trap. Take a step back in time and visit **Muckross Traditional Farms** (the entrance is on the opposite side of the car park to the house). Stroll up the lane (or ride the old bus) to visit three farms that demonstrate what Kerry farming was like in the 1930s before the advent of electricity and farming machinery. Chat with the farmers and their wives as they go about their daily work. Muckross House and its vast estate were given to the Irish nation by the Bourne family of California, who had a smaller, lakeside estate, Filoli, just south of San Francisco.

Believe everything you ever read about the magnificent beauty of the Killarney lakes, but realize that **Killarney**, not an attractive town, is absolutely packed with tourists during the summer season. If you would like additional views of the lakes, then a tour to Aghadoe Hill or a boat trip from Ross Castle should give you what you are looking for. Leave Killarney on the road to Tralee (N22) and turn left for the 5-kilometer drive to **Aghadoe**, where Killarney town, lakes, and mountains can all be seen from this vantage point. If you prefer a close look at the lake and its island, take the 90-minute boat tour of the lower lake, which leaves from the jetty alongside Ross Castle. Tickets for this trip can be purchased from the tourist office in town. **Ross Castle** has been restored and you can climb its steep, stone stairs to see what living in a castle was like.

Ladies' View, Killarney

SIDE TRIP UP THE GAP OF DUNLOE

*The road through the **Gap of Dunloe** (signposted from the Killorglin road just past the golf course) is a single-lane dirt track up a 6-kilometer ravine carved by glaciers. **Kate Kearney's Cottage** sits at the entrance to the ravine. Legend has it that Kate was a beautiful witch who drove men wild with desire—now her home is greatly enlarged as a* *coffee and souvenir shop. As you travel up the gap the dramatic setting is enhanced by the purple mountains on your left and **Macgillycuddy's Reeks** on your right.*

In the past I have recommended an evening drive up the gap to emerge on the N71, just west of Moll's Gap, and returning to Killarney with a quick stop at Ladies' View to admire the unparalleled views of the lakes of Killarney. Signs have been posted to discourage motor traffic. I recommend that you either park your car near Kate Kearney's cottage and walk, arrange for a jaunting car to take you up the gap or purchase a ticket at the tourist office for the Dero Tours day trip. This includes a shuttle service from your lodging to the gap, horse or jaunting car rides up the ravine, transportation by electric boat through the lakes of Killarney, and transportation back to your lodging.

Leaving Killarney, a two-hour drive will bring you to Limerick, but rather than taking a direct route, take the time to explore the lovely **Dingle Peninsula**. It's a very special place, a narrow promontory of harshly beautiful land and seascapes where the people are especially friendly and welcoming to strangers. The road from Killarney to Dingle town takes you northwest to **Castlemaine** where you follow the coast road west through **Inch** to Dingle town, the largest settlement on the peninsula (it's only an hour-and-a-half drive from Killarney to Dingle).

Leaving Killarney, a two-hour drive will bring you to Limerick, but rather than taking a direct route, take the time to explore the lovely **Dingle Peninsula**. It's a very special place, a narrow promontory of harshly beautiful land and seascapes where the people are especially friendly and welcoming to strangers. The road from Killarney to Dingle town takes you northwest to **Castlemaine** where you follow the coast road west through **Inch** to Dingle town, the largest settlement on the peninsula (it's only an hour-and-a-half drive from Killarney to Dingle).

Colorfully painted pubs, shops, and houses welcome you to **Dingle** (*An Daingean*) where fishing boats bob in the harbor unloading bountiful catches of fish and shellfish. It is not surprising that you find a great many excellent seafood restaurants here. After dinner, ask where you can go to hear traditional Irish music. Dingle's population is under 2,000, yet it has over 50 pubs, some of which double as shops—like **Foxy John's**, where you can buy hardware while enjoying a drink, and **McCarthy's** with its poetry readings. There are several interesting shops—**Brian de Staic's** jewelry store contains exquisite gold and silver jewelry inspired by Dingle's flora and ancient Celtic motifs.

The Dingle Peninsula

KEY

1. The Blasket Island Centre
2. Reask
3. Gallarus Oratory
4. Kilmalkedar Church
5. Loch a Duin
6. Mount Brandon
● Orientation/ Sightseeing

Plan to spend at least two nights on the peninsula to experience the beauty and tranquility offered by the unspoiled scenery of the spectacular beaches and rocky promontories that lie to the west of Dingle town. Take time to wander along the beaches or walk along the lanes, where fuchsia hedges divide the fields and friendly locals wave a salute of welcome, and to take the trip to the Blasket Islands. Because Irish is the official language of the peninsula, signposts are in Irish (though commercial maps are in English) so we give the Irish in parentheses to aid you in finding your way. We outline a route that will take you on a half-day drive around Slea Head. But for a real appreciation of the 2,000 archaeological sites of the Dingle Peninsula (peppered with lots of interesting stories), we recommend forsaking your car and taking one of **Sciuird's** minivan or walking tours. Michael and his dad, Timothy, offer tours that range from an hour's walk round Dingle town to visiting ancient, Ogham stones, wedge tombs, standing stones, and ring forts. (*Sciuird, email: collinskirrary@eircom.net, tel: 066 9151606*)

The road to Slea Head, signposted as **Slea Head Drive** (*Ceann Sléibhe*), twists and turns, following the contours of the increasingly rocky coast. Stunning seascapes present themselves, demanding that you pause just to admire the view. Several of the farms along the way have beehive stone huts and, for a small fee, the farmers will let you climb up to visit them. Conjecture has it that these small huts were used by early pilgrims traveling the St. Brendan's pilgrimage route. A large, white crucifix marks **Slea Head**, which affords the first view of the **Blasket Islands** (*Na Blascaodaí*), alternately sparkling like jewels in the blue ocean and disappearing under dark clouds a moment later.

Around the point, the scattered village of **Dunquin** (*Dún Chaoin*) and the **Blasket Island Centre** come into view. The building is impressive, with exhibits lining a long corridor that leads to an observatory overlooking the island's abandoned village. Remarkably, this tiny, isolated island abode produced an outpouring of music and writing. Three classics of Irish literature emerged with Peig Sayers' *Peig,* Thomas Crohan's *The Islandman*, and Maurice O'Sullivan's *Twenty Years a'Growing.* The islands have been uninhabited since 1953, when the last islanders evacuated their windswept homes. The center's large, airy dining room serves food and provides enticing island views.

Before you visit the center, take a left turn, park on the cliff top (opposite the two yellow bungalows), and walk down to Dunquin's **pier**, which sits away from the scattered village and is reached by a steep path that zigzags down the cliff. As you round the last twist, you see curraghs turned upside-down looking like giant, black beetles stranded high above the water line. Curraghs are fragile boats made of tarred canvas stretched over a wooden skeleton. St. Brendan is reputed to have discovered America in such a boat. In clear weather a ferry takes day-trip visitors to and from **Great Blasket Island**. The little village on the island is mostly in ruins, and paths wander amongst the fields where the hardy islanders struggled to earn a living—a café offers the only shelter.

On the road to **Ballyferriter** (*Balle an Fheirtearaigh*), the pottery of **Louis Mulcahy** makes an interesting stop. During the summer you can try your hand at throwing a pot, and thus gain an appreciation for how difficult it is. One kilometer after driving through **Ballyferriter** (*Balle an Fheirtearaigh*), an attractive little village with a couple of pubs, pass Tig Bhric (a pub and shop) on your right and make a right-hand turn (small signpost) to **Reask** (*Riasc*), an ancient monastic settlement with its large slab cross and foundations of beehive huts.

Returning to the main road, a couple of kilometers' drive brings you to the **Gallarus Oratory** (*Séipéilín Ghallarais*). Over 1,000 years ago many of St. Brendan's contemporaries lived on the Dingle Peninsula in unmortared, beehive-shaped stone huts called clochans. The most famous example is the Gallarus Oratory, a tiny church built not as a circle, but in the shape of an upturned boat. It has a small window at one end, a small door at the other, and is as watertight today as when it was built over 900 years ago. A privately run enterprise offers a little visitors' center and a café, and charges a fee to cross their land to visit the monument. If you would rather not pay a fee, drive up the adjacent, public road and the monument is signed a short walk to your left.

Arriving in the nearby village of **Múirioch,** turn right at the Y for **Kilmalkedar Church** (*Séipéal Chill Mhaolchéadair*). This now-roofless place of worship was built in the 12th century on the site of a 7th-century church. However, it dates back even further, for within the graveyard is a magnificent, early Christian cross, an ancient Ogham stone, and an intricately decorated sundial. Within the church stands a rare alphabet stone, which the monks used for teaching the alphabet. Locals refer to the little slit east window as the eye of the needle and folklore has it that if you climb through the window, you will surely marry within a year and a day.

Continuing uphill, the field to your right contains the ruins of the Chancellor's House. Park your car by the gate on the right that follows the little lane (not signposted) and walk into the farmer's field to examine the waist-high foundations of the **Caher Dorgan** *(Cathar Dairgáin)* ring fort with its beehive huts. On a clear day, you get a magnificent view of the Three Sisters, a line of three mountains that tumble into the sea.

Cresting the rise, you travel 5 kilometers of the Dingle Peninsula's straightest road, known as *An Bóthar Fada*—The Long Road. It must have seemed a very long road for farmers walking to town. In the distance, the entrance to Dingle's harbor is guarded by **Esk Tower**, built in 1847 by an English landlord to give paid work to the men of Dingle. Its giant wooden hand serves as a marker for fishermen to the entrance to the protected harbor.

NOTE: If you get lost on the peninsula's little lanes, ask a friendly local or follow signposts for *An Daingean*, Dingle town.

There are lots of interesting walks on the Dingle Peninsula. Two of the more unusual ones are following the **Way of St. Brendan**, and exploring the **Loch a Duin Valley**. The Way of St. Brendan is laid out on a map that you obtain at **Cloghane's** tiny tourist office. The route begins in nearby Brandon and follows a well-marked route that the saint supposedly took to the top of **Mount Brandon** (about five hours of walking). Cloghane's tourist office also sells a booklet that takes you on a self-guided tour through the Loch a Duin Valley (Sciuird also leads a walking tour). Beginning at the hut beside the road at the bottom of Connor Pass, this route leads you on a well-marked, three-hour walk through the valley's boglands. Structures associated with prehistoric habitation (2,000 B.C.), ritual, and agriculture, along with several kilometers of prehistoric field wall, still survive. The valley is also of interest to bird watchers, botanists, and geologists.

Leaving the Dingle Peninsula (signposted Tralee), the **Connor Pass** twists you upward to the summit, where a backward glance gives you a magnificent view of Dingle and its harbor. The view is spectacular, but there is no guarantee that you will see it—all will be green fields, blue sea and sky, until the mists roll in and everything vanishes. Follow the coast road through **Ballyduff**, **Stradbally**, and **Camp** to **Tralee**. (If you are heading for the Cliffs of Moher, take the N69 to the **Tarbert ferry**, which takes you across the River

Shannon.) At Tralee you join the main road (N21) for the drive to **Castleisland** and on to **Adare** with its charming row of thatched cottages and tree-lined streets. Less than an hour's drive will find you in **Limerick**, whose traffic-crowded streets can be avoided by taking the ring road signposted Ennis and Shannon Airport.

Dingle

The Southwest

The West

Céide Fields

Sligo

Bangor

N59

N59

Crossmolina   Ballina

Achill Island

Lough Conn   N17

Mulrany   Newport

Rosturk   N59   Castlebar

Westport

Louisburgh

Inishbofin Island

Leenane   Lough Mask

Cleggan

Letterfrack

Clifden   Lough Corrib

Oughterard   Aughnanure Castle

Roundstone   N59

Rossaveel   Galway

Dunguaire Castle

Aran Islands   Kilronan

Dún Aengus   Lisdoonvarna   Ballyvaughan   Thoor Ballylee

The Burren   Kilfenora   N18

Corofin

Ennis

Shannon Airport

Limerick

Belfast

Dublin

● Orientation/ Sightseeing

‑ ‑ ‑ Itinerary Route

— Roads

••• Alternative Route & Sidetrips

✈ Airport

The West

This itinerary takes you off the beaten tourist track through the wild, hauntingly beautiful scenery of Connemara, and County Mayo. Lying on the coast of County Clare, The Burren presents a vast landscape of smooth, limestone rocks—whose crevices are ablaze with rock roses, blue gentians, and all manner of Arctic and Alpine flowers in the spring and early summer. Otherwise, there are no trees, shrubs, rivers, or lakes—just bare "moonscapes" of rocks dotted with forts and ruined castles, tombs, and rock cairns. Traveling to Connemara, your route traces the vast, island-dotted Lough Corrib and traverses boglands and moorlands. Distant mountains fill the horizon and guide you to the coast, where gentle waves lap at rocky inlets sheltering scattered villages with whitewashed cottages dotting the landscape. Ireland's holy mountain, Croagh Patrick, and the windswept Achill Island leave a deep impression on the visitor.

Cliffs of Moher

Recommended Pacing: It is possible to tour the west in just a few days, but this beautiful area calls for you to linger. Our ideal would be one or two nights on or near The Burren, two or three nights in Connemara, and two or three nights near either Crossmolina or Sligo.

Leave **Limerick** in the direction of Ennis and Shannon airport and you soon arrive at **Bunratty Castle and Folk Park**. An interesting history and guide to the castle is available at the entrance. As the majority of castles in Ireland stand roofless and in ruins, it is a treat to visit a 15th-century castle that has been restored so beautifully. The authentic 14th- to 17th-century furniture in the rooms gives the castle a real lived-in feel. In the evenings, firelit banquets warmed with goblets of mead whisk visitors back to the days when the castle was young. In the castle grounds, a folk park contains several cottages, farmhouses, and a whole 19th-century village street of shops, houses, and buildings furnished appropriately for their era. The community is brought to life by costumed townspeople who bake, make butter, and tend the animals. **Bunratty Cottage**, opposite the castle, offers a wide range of handmade Irish goods, and just at the entrance to the park is **Durty Nelly's**, one of Ireland's most popular pubs, dating from the 1600s.

Just to the northwest lies the strangest landscape in Ireland, **The Burren**. Burren means "a rocky place" and this is certainly the case for, as far as the eye can see, this is a wilderness—a wilderness that is rich in archaeological sites (megalithic tombs, ring forts, and the remains of ancient huts) and strange rock formations whose tiny crevices are a mass of Arctic, Mediterranean, and Alpine flowers in springtime. Ludlow, one of Cromwell's generals, passing through the area in 1649, wrote, "There is not enough wood to hang a man, nor water to drown him, nor earth enough to bury him in."

Base yourself at either **Corofin** or **Ballyvaughan** (see *Places to Stay*) to explore this unique area. One of the most photographed sights, the **Poulnabrone Portal Tomb,** is found alongside the road between Corofin and Ballyvaughan.

To help you appreciate this unusual landscape, first visit The **Burren Display Centre** at **Kilfenora**, which offers a film on the geology and rare flora and fauna of the area.

Models explain the pattern of settlement and the geological makeup of the area, and show the non-botanist what to look for. Next to the Centre, the crumbling remains of Ladies Chapel has a glass roof sheltering three celtic crosses with symbolic carvings from the elements. A fourth cross is open to the elements in an adjacent field.

Turn right as you leave the interpretive center and left as you come to the main road to reach the **Cliffs of Moher**—the most spectacular section of the coastline—where towering cliffs rise above the pounding Atlantic Ocean. These majestic cliffs, stretching along 5 kilometers of the coast, are one of Ireland's most popular sights. The cliffs face due west, which means that the best time to see them is on a bright, summer evening. The visitors' center offers welcome shelter on cool and windy days. A short distance from the visitors' center, **O'Brien's Tower** (built in 1835 by Sir Cornelius O'Brien, Member of Parliament, for "strangers visiting the magnificent scenery of this neighborhood") marks the highest and most photographed point along the clifftops.

On leaving the cliffs, head north toward, but not into, Lisdoonvarna. Follow the coastal road around Black Head, where the rocky Burren spills into Galway Bay—to Ballyvaughan, where you turn right following signs for the **Aillwee Caves** on the bluff above. The visitors' center is so cleverly designed that it is hard to distinguish it from the surrounding gray landscape. Beneath the eerie "moonscape" of the Burren lie vast caves, streams, and lakes. You can take a tour through a small section of these underground caverns. The first is called Bear Haven because the bones of a brown bear that died long ago were found here. In other chambers, you see limestone cascades, stalactites, and stalagmites before the tour ends at the edge of an underground river. Remember to dress warmly, for it's cool in the caves.

Retrace your steps a short distance down the road towards Ballyvaughan and take the first turn left, passing Gregans Castle hotel and up Corkscrew Hill, a winding road that takes you from a lush, green valley to the gray, rocky landscape above. Take the first turn to the left and you come to **Cahermacnaghten**, a ring fort that was occupied until the 18th century. You enter via a medieval two-story gateway, and the foundations of buildings of similar date can be seen inside the stone wall.

Some 7 kilometers farther south, you come to another ring fort, **Ballykinvarga**. You have to walk several hundred meters before you see the Iron-Age fort surrounded by its defensive, pointed stones known as *chevaux de frise*, a term derived from a military expression describing how Dutch Frisians used spikes to impede attackers. Ireland has three other such forts, of which the two most impressive are found on the Aran Islands.

When you leave The Burren, head directly for the coast and follow it east (N67) to **Kinvarra**, a pretty village with boats bobbing in the harbor and small rocky islands separating it from the expanse of Galway Bay. On the outskirts of the village, the restored **Dunguaire Castle** has a craft shop and, on summer evenings, hosts medieval banquets.

 From the castle car park, turn towards the village and immediately take a left-hand turn (opposite the castle entrance) for the 5-kilometer drive to **Ardrahan**, where you turn right on the N18 and, after 6 kilometers, left for the 2-kilometer drive to **Thoor Ballylee**. William Butler Yeats bought this 13th-century tower house and cottage in 1917 and it was his summer home for 11 years. The cozy, thatched cottage is now a bookshop. An audio-visual presentation tells of Yeats's artistic and political achievements. Two floors of the tower are sparsely furnished as they were in his occupancy. By pressing a green button on each room's wall you receive information and hear excerpts of his poetry. Leaving Thoor Ballylee, retrace your steps to the N18 for a 24-kilometer drive to **Galway**.

SIDE TRIP TO THE ARAN ISLANDS

*If you are planning to visit the **Aran Islands**, take the coastal route through Spiddal to **Rossaveel** where two ferry companies operate a shuttle service to **Kilronan** on **Inishmore**, the largest of the three Aran Islands. Until a decade or so ago, time had stood still here and the way of life and the culture of the islanders had changed little. Now their traditional dress comes out only for TV cameras and special occasions, and their traditional way of life has been replaced by a more profitable one—tourism. In the summertime, more than double the population of the islands arrives on Inishmore as day-trippers. When you arrive, visit the Tourist Information Centre by the harbor to discuss* *the cost of horse and trap, bicycle (there are plenty of shops where you can rent bikes), and minibus transportation. The barren landscape is closely related to that of The Burren: sheer cliffs plunge into the pounding Atlantic Ocean along the southern coast, while the north coast flattens out with shallow, rock-ringed, sandy beaches. You will have no difficulty obtaining transportation to* **Dún Aengus** *(about 8 kilometers from the harbor), the best known of the island's stone forts, believed to date from the early Celtic period some two to three thousand years ago. It has sheer cliffs at its back and is surrounded by pointed boulders designed to twist ankles and skin shins. Despite the hordes of visitors scrambling over its walls and stones, Dún Aengus is remarkably well preserved. With four stone forts, remains of stone huts, high crosses, and ruined churches to examine, the archaeologically minded could spend many days with detailed map in hand exploring the islands.*

Those who are not island bound should follow signs for Clifden (N59) around Galway. Leaving the town behind, the road is straight and well paved, but a tad bouncy if you try to go too fast. Accommodation signs for nearby Oughterard alert you to watch for a right-hand turn to **Aughnanure Castle**. Approaching the castle, you may be greeted, as we were, by a friendly family of goats snoozing on the wooden footbridge before the castle gates. Aughnanure Castle was the stronghold of the ferocious O'Flahertys, who launched attacks on Galway town until their castle was destroyed by English forces in 1572. The clan regained their castle for a period of time until wars with Cromwell and William of Orange saw them expelled again. Nearby **Oughterard** is a pleasant, bustling town, "the gateway to Connemara," whose main street has several, attractive shops. A stay here affords the opportunity for fishing and exploring the island-dotted Lough Corrib by boat.

Clifden

Beyond Oughterard, you plunge into Connemara past the **Twelve Bens** mountains, which dominate the wild, almost treeless landscape of bogs, lakes, and rivers; a landscape that is ever being changed by the dashing clouds that rush in from the Atlantic. Apart from the occasional craft shop, there are no houses until you reach **Clifden** (see listings) on the Atlantic coast (N59, 80 kilometers). Clifden is the major market town of Connemara and the home of the annual Connemara Pony Show (*third week in August*). The town presents a gay face with shopfronts painted in bright hues of red, blue, yellow, and green. Craft and tourist shops alternate with the butchers, the hardware store, pubs, and restaurants. On Market Street, you find the **Connemara Walking Centre** where you can buy booklets on the locale and sign up for one of the walking tours that vary from an interesting stroll through the Roundstone bogs—great walking amongst lakes full of otters and interesting plant life—to the demanding climb up one half of the great Glanhoaghan Horseshoe in the stark Twelve Bens mountains.

SIDE TRIP TO ROUNDSTONE

*To the south of Clifden, the road has more views of sea than land, as little boats bob in rocky inlets and cottages gaze westward across tiny islands. The road passes the marshy area where Alcock and Brown crash-landed after the first transatlantic flight in 1919 (commemorated by a monument about 500 meters from the main road). Via **Ballinaboy**, **Ballyconneely**, and **Roundstone**, the sweeping seascapes that this route presents are so compelling that it is difficult to concentrate on the driving.*

SIDE TRIP TO INISHBOFIN ISLAND

*If the weather is fine, a delightful day trip can be taken to **Inishbofin Island**. The Inishbofin boat leaves from Cleggan pier at 11:30 am, returning at 5 pm (the crossing takes less than an hour). Be at **Cleggan** pier half an hour before sailing time and buy your ticket at the Pier Bar. Sailings depend on weather conditions, so it's best to phone ahead to verify departure times. The boat sails into the sheltered harbor presided over by the remains of a Cromwellian castle, and you wade ashore at a cluster of houses that make up the island's main settlement. Many islanders have left in search of greener pastures and their cottages have fallen into disrepair, but those who remain eke out a hard living from the land and the sea. As you walk down lanes edged with wild fuchsias and brightly colored wildflowers, whitewashed farmhouses appear and you see fields dotted with handmade haystacks. At the far side of the island, a row of cottages fronts the beach, one of them housing a welcoming little café, where you can have lunch or tea before walking back to the harbor to take the evening boat back to Cleggan.*

Clifden stands just outside the **Connemara National Park**, which covers 5,000 acres of mountain, heath, and bog—there are no pretty gardens or verdant woodlands. The video in the visitors' center gives a beautiful introduction to the park, which has wonderful hiking trails. If you want to tackle the smaller paths leading into the Twelve Bens mountains, consider joining one of the guided walks that begin at the visitors' center (four of the Twelve Bens, including Benbaum, the highest, are found in the park). Two signposted nature trails start at the center: one leads you through Ellis Wood while the other takes you into rougher terrain.

Leaving Clifden to the north, the N59 passes the much-photographed **Kylemore Abbey**. Originally built by a wealthy Englishman in the 19th century, this grand home, surrounded by greenery and fronting a lake, passed into the hands of Benedictine nuns who have a school here. You'll find ample parking (lots of coaches) and a large restaurant and gift shop. You can walk beside the lake to the abbey, where in summer the library is open to visitors. In the grounds, you can visit the restored Gothic chapel with its pretty, sandstone interior and different-colored, marble pillars. Follow the shore of **Killary Harbor**, the longest and most picturesque fjord in Ireland, to **Leenane**, a little village nestled at the head of the inlet. Continue along the shoreline and take the first turn to the left, signposted as a scenic route to Westport via Louisburgh. This interesting side road gently winds you along the sea lough to **Delphi**, an area of pools and loughs amongst some of the highest and wildest mountains in the west. Acres of woodlands offer shelter and there is not a bungalow in sight. The Marquis of Sligo built a lodge here in 1840 and called it "Delphi" because it reminded him of Delphi in Greece. After falling into dereliction, the house and estate were bought by the Mantles, who welcome guests to their restored home (see listing under Leenane).

Leaving Delphi, the isolated mountain road takes you along the shore of **Doo Lough** at the foot of **Mweelrea Mountain** and on through wild, remote scenery to **Louisburgh**; where, turning towards Westport, the summit of the conical-shaped **Croagh Patrick** (Ireland's most famous mountain) comes into view. Swirling mists substantiate its mystical place in Irish history. It was after St. Patrick spent the 40 days of Lent atop its rocky summit in 441 that the mountain became sacred to Christians. Every year thousands of penitential pilgrims begin their climb to the oratory at the summit at dawn on the last Sunday in July, several going barefoot up the stony track. The ritual involves stopping at three stations and reciting prayers. No climbing skills are needed as it's a well-worn path to the top and, on a clear day, a walk to the summit affords a panoramic view across Clew Bay to Achill Island.

Croagh Patrick

Nearby **Westport** lies on the shore of Clew Bay and is unique amongst Irish towns because it was built following a pre-designed plan. The architect walled the river and lined the riverside malls with lime trees and austere Georgian homes, forming a most delightful thoroughfare. There's a buzz to the town and, on a sunny day, you can enjoy a drink at the tables and chairs outside **Geraghtey's Bar** and **Grand Central**, on the Octagon (the heart of the town with a granite pillar in the center of the square). At **Clew Bay Heritage Centre** on Westport Quay, postcards and old photographs show the town as it was at the turn of the last century. There is also a genealogical research center and a display on the maritime traditions of Westport.

From Westport, the most direct route to Sligo is by way of the broad, well-paved, fast N5, and N17. However, if the weather is clear and bright, it is a delightful drive from Westport to Sligo via **Newport**, **Achill Island**, **Crossmolina**, and **Ballina**.

Achill Island is Ireland's largest offshore island. Traditionally, the Achill islanders traveled to Scotland as migrant farmworkers during the summer; but now the population that has not been enticed away by emigration, remains to garner a meager living from a harsh land. This was the home of the infamous British Captain Boycott; who gave his name to the English language when tenants "boycotted" him for his excessive rents during the potato famine. Today, this island holds the allure that belongs to wild and lonely places: in sunshine it is glorious; but in torrential rain, it is a grim and depressing place. On the island, take the first turn to your left, signposted for the windswept **Atlantic Drive**, where you drive along the tops of rugged cliffs carved by the pounding Atlantic Ocean far below. The "drive" ends at **Knockmore** where scattered houses shelter from the biting winds.

Returning to Mulrany, turn north on the N59 for the 32-kilometer drive across boglands, where vast quantities of turf are harvested by mechanical means, to **Bangor** and on to **Crossmolina, Ballina,** and **Sligo**. The many sightseeing opportunities in the Sligo area are outlined in the following itinerary.

SIDE TRIP TO CÉIDE FIELDS

*From Ballina, you can detour north 20 kilometers to Ballycastle and drive another 8 kilometers east to the great cliffs of **Downpatrick Head**, where the Stone-Age settlements at **Céide Fields** (pronounced "kay-jeh") are being excavated. Under the peat has been unearthed the most extensive Stone-Age settlement in the world, with walls older than the pyramids, a vast site which once supported a community of over 10,000 people. Wander round a portion of the archaeological dig, and enjoy an audio-visual presentation and a cup of tea in the pyramid-shaped visitors' center. The surrounding cliffs are amongst the most magnificent you will see in Ireland. Retrace your steps to Ballycastle, and take the*

*R314 through **Killala** (a workaday village whose skyline is punctuated by an ancient, round tower) to **Ballina** where you turn left for **Sligo**.*

From the Sligo area—you can go into Northern Ireland, continue north on the following itinerary, or return south. If you travel south, consider visiting either **Ballintubber Abbey**, a beautifully restored church dating back to 1216, or the village of **Knock**. A religious apparition seen on the gable of the village church in 1879, and some hearty promotion, has led to the development of Knock as a religious pilgrimage site and a tourist venue. A giant basilica stands next to the little church, a large complex of religious souvenir shops sits across the road, and nearby Knock airport has a runway capable of providing landing facilities for large jets. Surrounded as it is by narrow country lanes, this sophisticated complex seems very out of place in rural Ireland.

The North

- ● Orientation/Sightseeing
- – – Itinerary Route
- — Roads
- ··· Alternative Route & Sidetrips
- ✈ Airport

Tory Island

Rosguill Peninsula

Rosapenna

Glenveagh Castle

Dunglow

Letterkenny

N56

N13

N56

Derry

Limavady

A2

A2

Giant's Causeway

Ballintoy

Carrick-a-Rede Rope Bridge

Bushmills

Coleraine

Torr Head

Glenariff Forest Park

Cushendun

Cushendall

A26

Carnlough

Larne

Glencolumbkille

Ardara

Carrick

Bruckless

Donegal

N15

N15

Carrickfergus

A2

M2

Belfast

✈

Belleek

Lough Erne

Drumcliff

Enniskillen

Sligo

N16

Marble Arch Caves

Belfast

Dublin

The North

The northernmost reaches of Ireland hold special appeal. Herein lies the countryside that inspired the moving poetry of William Butler Yeats. Beyond Donegal, narrow roads twist and turn around the wild, rugged coastline of County Donegal, where villagers weave their tweeds and Irish is often the spoken language and that written on the signposts. The Folk Village Museum at Glencolumbkille, with its authentically furnished, thatch-topped cottages, demonstrates the harsh living conditions of the far north. Crossing into Northern Ireland, the honeycomb columns of the Giant's Causeway signpost the Antrim coast full of cliffs, lush green headlands, and beautiful views.

Dunluce Castle

Recommended Pacing: Two or three nights around Sligo and Donegal, a night near Glenveagh National Park (to permit a leisurely visit), and two nights along the Antrim coast will give you time to explore this lovely area.

The county and town of **Sligo** are ever mindful of William Butler Yeats, and the whole area is promoted as being Yeats country. If you are an ardent admirer of the poet, you will want to visit the **County Museum**, which has a special section about his poetry and writing. Base yourself near the town for several days—**Ballymote** and **Riverstown** are our accommodation choices in the *Places to Stay* section. The countryside is very pretty and there is enough sightseeing to keep you busy for a week.

SIDE TRIP TO CARROWMORE AND CARROWKEEL

*Seven kilometers to the southwest of Sligo town, sitting in fields on either side of a narrow country lane, are the megalithic tombs of **Carrowmore**. Wander amongst the cows and explore the little stone circles and larger dolmens which make up what is reputed to be the largest Bronze-Age cemetery in Europe. Farther inland take the Boyle road (N4) 30 kilometers south of Sligo to Castlebaldwin, where you turn right following signposts for Carrowkeel. At the end of a mountain track, you come to **Carrowkeel**, a 4,000-year-old passage tomb cemetery. There are 13 cairns covering passage tombs, while the 14th is a long cairn. One of the tombs can be entered (backwards) and it is claimed that, on the summer solstice, the setting sun lights up the main chamber.*

SIDE TRIP AROUND LOUGH GILL

*A half-day sightseeing trip from Sligo can be taken by driving around Lough Gill, visiting Parke's Castle, and enjoying a meal at Markree Castle. Leave Sligo to the north and follow signposts for Enniskillen, Lough Derg, and Dromohair, which bring you to the northerly shore of **Lough Gill**. Glimpses of the lough through the trees give way to stunning lough views as the road hugs the shore and arrives at **Parke's Castle**, a fortified manor house whose ramparts and cottages (tearooms) have been restored. In summer, you can take a boat trip on the lake which takes you around **Inishfree Island**. Leaving the castle, follow the lough into **Dromohair** where you pick up the Sligo road. After 5 kilometers, when the road divides, take a single-track lane to the right, which leads you down to the lakeside where John O'Connel's rowboat is tied to the pier. He lives by the lake and is sometimes available to row you to Inishfree Island. Returning to the main road, it's a short drive to **Collooney**, where you can partake of lunch or afternoon tea at **Markree Castle**.*

Leaving Sligo, travel north along the N15 to **Drumcliff Churchyard**, which has to be the most visited graveyard in Ireland. Handily there's an excellent café. William Butler Yeats is buried here under the epitaph he composed, "Cast a cold eye on life, on death. Horseman, pass by!" In the background is the imposing **Benbulben Mountain**. Beyond the village, a left turn leads to **Lissadell,** home of the Gore-Booth sisters with whom Yeats was friendly. The 1830s Greek Revival-style house is full of curiosities and quite a sight to behold, but in need of an injection of capital to prevent its decay. While the sisters belonged to the landed gentry, Eva went on to become a poet and an important member of the suffragette movement. Constance was a commander in the 1916 uprising and the first elected female Labour Party M.P. Sir Henry Gore-Booth went off with his butler to explore the Antarctic in the 1880s. The bear that the butler shot is on the stairs.

Leaving Lissadell, continue north on the N15 for the 60-kilometer drive to Donegal, or follow a more circuitous route through Northern Ireland.

ALTERNATIVE ROUTE TO DONEGAL

*From Drumcliff churchyard, return towards Sligo and, at **Rathcormack**, turn left through the village of **Drum** to join the N16 as it travels east towards **Enniskillen**. Cross into Northern Ireland and take the first turn to your right following signposts to **Marble Arch Caves**. This extensive network of limestone chambers (billed as "over 300 million years of history") is most impressive. The tour includes an underground boat journey, walks through large illuminated chambers, galleries hung with remarkable stalactites, and a "Moses Walk" along a man-made passage through a lake where your feet are at the bottom of the pool and your head is at the same level as the water. Remember to dress warmly and take a sweater. It is best to telephone in advance because, if there has been a lot of rain, the caves are closed.*

*Leaving the hilltop cave complex, follow signposts for Enniskillen for 7 kilometers to **Florence Court**, an 18th-century mansion that was once the home of the Earls of Enniskillen. The opulent mansion is elegantly furnished and famous for the impressive rococo plasterwork on the ceilings. On leaving Florence Court, do **not** go into Enniskillen, but turn left onto the A46, following the scenic southern shore of **Lough Erne** for the 38-kilometer drive to Belleek.*

***Belleek**, on the far north shore of the lough, is famous for its ornate, creamy pottery: porcelain festooned with shamrocks or delicate, spaghetti-like strands woven into trellis-like plates. You can tour the visitors' center and then browse at the factory shop. Crossing back into the Republic, head for **Ballyshannon** and follow the wide N15 north for 23 kilometers to Donegal.*

Glencolumbkille

Donegal is a busy, bustling place, laid out around a diamond-shaped area surrounded by shops. Donegal is one of the best places to buy tweed goods—**Magees** sells a variety. The **Four Masters Bookshop** is a handy place to stock up on reading material. The ruins of **Donegal Castle** (open to the public), built in the 16th century by Hugh O'Donell, stand beside the Diamond.

Take the N56 west, hugging the coast, through **Dunkineely** and **Bruckless** to **Killybegs**, Ireland's major fishing port. Large trawlers from all over the world have replaced family fishing boats in the working harbor of this most enjoyable town. As you move west from Killybegs, the roads become more difficult, the landscape more rugged, the signposts less frequent, and—to complicate things—they are often written in Irish (Irish names are referenced in parentheses).

If the weather is fine, you can enjoy some spectacular scenery by following the brown signs that indicate a coastal route from **Kilcar** to **Carrick** (*An Charraig*), where you turn left (in the center of the village opposite the pub) for **Telin** (*Teilean*) and follow the brown signs for **Bunglar** and The Cliffs. As the narrow road winds up, down, and around the rocky, rolling landscape; you see several examples of traditional Irish cottages with small, thatched, pony-cart barns huddled next to them. The road narrows to a single track taking you along the very edge of the headlands to a viewpoint that overlooks the spot where the **Slieve League Cliffs** plummet into the sea. Walkers will love the magnificent walks along the headlands. This is not a trip to be taken in inclement weather.

Retrace your steps to Carrick and turn left towards **Glencolumbkille** (*Gleann Cholaim Cille*). The road enters the Owenwee Valley where you climb before descending into the glen. Drive through the scattered village to **Glencolumbkille Folk Village Museum** at the water's edge. Glencolumbkille is a place that gives one an appreciation of the survival of a people who endured hardship, famine, and debilitating emigration. By the 1960s, emigration was threatening to turn Glencolumbkille into a ghost town. In an effort to create some jobs, the parish priest, Father McDyer, formed a cooperative of the remaining local residents to develop a tourist industry by building a folk museum and holiday homes, and by encouraging local crafts. Tucked against a rocky hillside, the cottages that comprise the folk museum are grouped to form a traditional, tiny, village (*clachan*). Each cottage is a replica of those lived in by local people in each of three successive centuries. The thick, thatched roofs are tied down with heavy rope and anchored with stones, securing them from the harsh Atlantic winds. Inside, the little homes are furnished with period furniture and utensils. Locals guide you through the houses and give you snippets of local history. A handicraft shop sells Irish cottage crafts and the adjacent tearoom serves scones and piping hot tea.

Leaving Glencolumbkille, the narrow road climbs and dips through seemingly uninhabited, rugged countryside, where the views are often obscured by swirling mists as you climb the Glengesh Pass before dropping down into **Ardara**.

The road skirts the coast and brings you to the twin fishing villages of **Portnoo** and **Nairn**, set amongst isolated beaches that truly have an "end-of-the-earth" quality about them. A short drive brings you to **Maas**, where you travel an extremely twisty road to the Gweebarra bridge taking you to **Lettermacaward** (*Leitir Mhic An Bhaird*) and on to **Dungloe** (*An Globhan Liath*). Nearby in **Burtonport** (*Ailt An Chorain*) more salmon and lobster are landed than at any other port. From here you drive north to **Kincasslagh**, and then it's on to **Annagary**, both tiny little communities that pride themselves on speaking the Irish language. A combination of wild, untamed scenery, villages that seem untouched by the 20th century, and narrow, curving roads in general disrepair, gives the feeling that the passage of time stopped many years ago in this isolated corner of Ireland.

Rejoin the N56 just south of **Gweedore** (*Gaoth Dobhair*) and follow it for a short distance as it swings inland paralleling a sea loch. As the main road swings to the right, continue straight up the mountain, following a narrow, winding road that brings you across peat bogs and purple, heather-covered moorlands inhabited only by sheep—to **Glenveagh National Park**, Ireland's largest, most natural, and most beautiful park. At its center lies a sheltered glen with a lake and mighty castle. The **Glenveagh Visitors' Centre** is well signposted and well disguised, being sunk into the ground with its roof camouflaged by peat and heather. There are displays, an audio-visual program, and a café (there's another at the castle), and it is here that you leave your car to take the minibus around the lake to **Glenveagh Castle** and its gardens. The heather and rose gardens, the rhododendrons, the laurels and pines, and busts and statues are all lovingly maintained, but the walled kitchen garden is especially memorable, with its profusion of flowers and tidy rows of vegetables divided by narrow, grass walkways. Surrounding this oasis of cultivated beauty are thousands of acres of wild countryside, where the largest herd of red deer in Ireland roam. Glenveagh Castle was built in 1870 by John Adair, using his American wife's money, in a fanciful gothic design that was popular in the later part of the century. The rooms have been beautifully restored and, for a small fee, you can tour the house (arrive by 2 pm if you're traveling in July and August). The Glenveagh estate was sold to the nation by the castle's second owner, Henry McIlhenny, who is largely responsible for the design of the gardens.

Leaving the national park, turn right across the desolate boglands and heather-clad hills—your destination is **Glebe House and Gallery** (6 kilometers away) near the village of **Churchhill**. Derek Hill gave his home, Glebe House, and his art collection to the state, which remodeled the outbuildings to display his fine collection of paintings. Among the 300 paintings are works by Picasso, Bonnard, Yeats, Annigoni, and Pasmore. The decoration in the house includes William Morris papers and textiles, Victoriana, Donegal folk art, and Japanese and Islamic art. There is a tearoom in the courtyard.

SIDE TRIP TO THE ROSGUILL PENINSULA AND TORY ISLAND

*If you would like to experience more Donegal coastal landscape, you can do no better than tour the **Rosguill Peninsula**, whose 25-kilometer Atlantic drive traces a wild, coastal route from **Rosapenna** through **Downies** and **Doagh** to **Tranarossan Bay** and back to Rosapenna. The road goes up and down, most of the time high above the ocean, then sweeps down to white, sandy beaches.*

*If you follow the coastal road west through **Gortahawk**, you come to **Meenlaragh** where you take the ferry to **Tory Island**, a windswept island where the inhabitants eke out a hard life farming and fishing. Sailing times of the ferryboat depend on the weather. If you want to visit the island, contact the Post Office in Meenlaragh.*

Giant's Causeway

From Glebe House, it is a 16-kilometer drive to **Letterkenny**. From the town, your route into Northern Ireland is well signposted to **Derry**. The N13 becomes the A2 as you cross the border and the pound sterling becomes the currency. Skirt Derry city on the **Foyle Bridge**, then follow the A2 to **Limavady** and the A37 for 21 kilometers to **Coleraine**.

Bushmills and the Giant's Causeway are well signposted from the outskirts of Coleraine. (One of the delights of traveling in Northern Ireland is that the roads are well paved and the signposting frequent and accurate.) **Bushmills** (see listings) is famous for its whiskey—a whiskey spelled with an "e"—of which Special Old Black Bush is the best. A tour of the factory demonstrates how they turn barley and water into whiskey and rewards you with a sample of the classic drink to fortify you for your visit to the nearby Giant's Causeway.

In the last century, the **Giant's Causeway** was thought to be one of the wonders of the world. Formed from basaltic rock, which cooled and split into regular, prismatic shapes, it stepped out to sea to build an irregular honeycomb of columns some 70,000,000 years ago. More romantic than scientific fact is the legend that claims the causeway was built by the Irish giant, Finn MacCool, to get at his rival in Scotland. Do not expect the columns to be tall, for they are not—it is their patterns that make them interesting, not their size.

The first stop on a visit to the causeway is the **Giant's Causeway Centre**, where the facts and legends about the causeway are well presented in an audio-visual theater. A minibus takes you to the head of the causeway, where you follow the path past formations called "Honeycomb," "Wishing Well," "Giant's Granny," "King and his Nobles," "Port na Spaniagh" (where gold and silver treasure from the Spanish Armada ship, *Girona,* was found in 1967), and "Lovers' Leap" and then up the wooden staircase to the headlands, where you walk back to the visitors' center along the clifftops. (It's a 5-kilometer walk and you can truly say you have seen the causeway, if you complete the circuit.)

Leaving the causeway, turn right along the coast to visit the ruins of the nearby **Dunluce Castle**, a romantic ruin clinging to a wave-lashed cliff with a great cave right underneath. This was the main fort of the Irish MacDonnells, chiefs of Antrim. It fell into ruin after the kitchen (and cooks!) fell into the sea during a storm.

Retrace your route down the B146 and, at the causeway gates, turn left along the coast road. Watch carefully for a small plaque at the side of the road pointing out the very meager ruins of **Dunseverick Castle**. Dunseverick was at the northernmost end of the Celtic road where the Celts crossed to and from Scotland.

Shortly after joining the A2, turn left for **Port Braddon**. The road winds down to the sea where a hamlet of gaily painted houses and a church nestles around a sheltered harbor. As you stand in front of the smallest church in Ireland, the long, sandy beaches of **Whitepark Bay** stretch before you.

Carrick-a-Rede Rope Bridge

Farther along the coast, a narrow road winds down to the very picturesque **Ballintoy Harbour**, a sheltered haven for boats surrounded by small, jagged, rocky islands. At the first road bend after leaving Ballintoy village, turn sharp left for the **Carrick-a-Rede Rope Bridge**. This is one of the famous things to do in Ireland: walk high above the sea across a narrow, swinging bridge of planks and ropes that joins a precipitous cliff to a rocky island. Hardy fishermen, whose cottages and nets nestle in a sheltered cleft on the island and whose fragile wooden boats bob in the ocean below, still use the bridge.

Life in the nearby holiday town of **Ballycastle** centers around the beach, fishing, and golf. Cross the river and turn onto the A2 to **Ballyvoy**. If the weather is clear, turn left for the scenic drive to Cushendun around **Torr Head**. The narrow road, barely wide enough for two cars to pass, switches back across the headlands and corkscrews down the cliffside, offering spectacular views of the rugged coastline and the distant Mull of Kintyre in Scotland.

Nestled by the seashore, the pretty village of **Cushendun** has a National Trust Shop, an excellent place to buy high-quality souvenirs. When you leave Cushendun, the landscape softens and the road, thankfully, returns to a more manageable width. You are now entering the **Glens of Antrim**, where lush, green fields and a succession of beautiful views present themselves. At **Cushendall** you can detour into **Glenariff Forest Park**, the queen of the glens with a series of waterfalls plunging down a gorge traversed by a scenic path crossing rustic bridges. Thackeray described this glen as "Switzerland in miniature."

After your return to the coast road, **Carnlough**, a pretty seaside and fishing town, soon comes into view, its little white harbor full of bobbing boats. The **Londonderry Arms** was once a coaching inn and now is a hotel and restaurant.

Nearby **Glenarm** is the oldest of the coastal villages, dating back to the time of King John. The pseudo-gothic castle is the home of the Earl of Antrim, part of whose demesne, **Glenarm Forest**, climbs up from the glen and is open to the public.

Limestone cliffs present themselves as you approach **Larne**, a sizable seaport whose Viking origins are lost amongst more modern commercial developments. Wend your way through this busy port town, following the A2 to **Whitehead**. Nearby **Carrickfergus** is the oldest town in Northern Ireland. **Carrickfergus Castle**, a sturdy Norman castle overlooking the boat-filled harbor, was built as a stronghold in 1178 by John de Courcy after his invasion of Ulster; then taken by King John after a siege in 1210; fell to the Scots in 1316; and was captured by the French in 1760. Life-sized models and a film recreate the castle's turbulent past.

Leaving Carrickfergus, a 12-kilometer drive along the A2 and M2/M1 whisks you through, or into, **Belfast** (see listings), where the A1 will take you south through **Newry** and into the Republic. Or, if you are staying near the Antrim coast for several days of leisurely sightseeing, take the M2 to the A26, which quickly returns you to that area.

Carrickfergus Castle

The North

Places to Stay

The Dunraven Arms stands on the broad main street of this attractive town. With its sharply dressed staff, check-in desk, and lovely bedrooms it is has more the feel of a country house than a hostelry. Smartly decorated throughout, its attractive antique furniture adds to the old-world feeling. The large, informal bar is a gathering place for locals and residents alike, but if you want a few quiet moments, there are several quiet lounges with comfortable chairs overlooking the garden. While the bedrooms in the old hostelry have lots of character we also enjoy the luxurious rooms in the new wings that stretches down long corridors behind the inn into the garden. We love their spaciousness, large bathrooms and garden views. There's a good few of them that have antique four poster beds and fireplaces as well. The brasserie style dining room serves well priced food. There's always a traditional roast on the trolley to be carved at your table. For more casual dining visit the hotel's cozy restaurant, The Inn Between, in a quaint thatched cottage across the street. Enjoy the health center with its swimming pool, gymnasium and array of spa treatment rooms. The hotel specializes in making golfing, equestrian, and fishing arrangements for guests. *Directions:* Adare is on the N21, 40 km from Shannon airport, which makes it an ideal first or last stop in Ireland if you are traveling in the southwest.

DUNRAVEN ARMS
Owners: Louis & Bryan Murphy
Adare, Co. Limerick, Ireland
Tel: 061 605900, Fax: 061 396541
90 Rooms, Double: €190–€335*
*Breakfast not included: €20
*Service: 12.5%
Dinner: €45–€50
Open: all year, Credit cards: all major
Inn

Just down a country lane from the charming little ferry that plies its way to Waterford across the Barrow estuary, Dunbrody House was the onetime home of the Marquis of Donegal. Catherine and Kevin Dundon have transformed it from a private house to stylish top-class hotel complete with spa and cookery school. Kevin and his team produce food that is as exquisite to look at as it is gorgeous to eat. The house is a delightful blend of contemporary and country house—lots of scrumptious public rooms and some particularly spacious bedrooms, such as 300 with it's French windows opening up to the garden. Top of the line bathrooms are the order of the day and the house is wheelchair friendly. A resident corgi and labrador are on hand to escort you on invigorating walks that encompass terrific views of the Barrow Estuary. Be sure to visit the hens and stroll around the large organic fruit and vegetable gardens. Explore the wild and beautiful Hook Peninsula, visiting Europe's oldest lighthouse, and take the ferry to Waterford and its famous crystal factory. *Directions:* From Wexford take the R733 to Arthurstown. Dunbrody House is on your left as you approach the village. If arriving from Waterford, take the Passage East Ferry to Ballyhack. Turn right off the ferry and go 2 km (through Arthurstown) to Dunbrody House, which is on your right as you go up the hill.

DUNBRODY HOUSE
Owners: Catherine & Kevin Dundon
Arthurstown, Co. Wexford, Ireland
Tel: 051 389600, Fax: 051 389601
22 Rooms, Double: €240–€400
7 Suites: €395–€550
Dinner: €65
Open: all year, Credit cards: all major
Ireland's Blue Book
Country House Hotel

The Wicklow Mountains offer some of the finest walks in Ireland and there is no finer place to stay in the area than Ballyknocken House. Hospitality is Catherine Fulvio's keynote, with good baking and cooking providing the backbone for fine evening meals and decadent breakfasts. The house has been completely renovated and returned it to its original 1850s style so that it has all the charm of days gone by along with 21st-century plumbing. Five bedrooms have Victorian tubs with showers. All rooms are named after local places, the pronunciation of which may prove challenging! My favorites are Knocknaphrumpha and Aghowle at the front of the house with views over the garden. Catherine has a cooking school in the adjacent renovated milking sheds and guests often book one of her hour long classes on the baking of brown bread, scones and soda bread. If you want to stay for several days consider renting the two bedroom apartment over the cookery school. The Wicklow Way, Ireland's famous hill-walking route, is close by. If you are not up to long walks, the dogs will accompany you through the hills behind the farm—but be sure to have directions with you as they have a habit of depositing you at a neighbor's farm! *Directions:* Take the N11 south from Dublin towards Wicklow for 42 km to Ashford (just before Rathnew). Turn right immediately after the Petrol station up a steep hill and follow this road for almost 5 km to Ballyknocken House on your right.

BALLYKNOCKEN HOUSE
Owners: Catherine & Claudio Fulvio
Ashford
Glenealy, Co. Wicklow, Ireland
Tel: 040 444627, Fax: 040 444696
7 Rooms, Double: €118–€135
1 Apartment: €500–€750 weekly
Dinner: €39–€45 (not Sun or Mon)
Open: Feb to Dec, Credit cards: MC, VS
B&B & Self Catering

Bagenalstown is sometimes signposted Muine Bheag, which can lead to a certain amount of confusion in reaching Kilgraney House. But the effort put into finding it is worthwhile, for this is not your run-of-the-mill Irish country house—it's more like "Architectural Digest" than "Country Life." With its crisp lines and whimsical touches, the decor is the brainchild of your hosts, designers Bryan Leech and Martin Marley. After working abroad, Bryan and Martin returned to Ireland. Kilgraney House was put together with a touch of whimsy and artistic flair, traditional Irish antiques being added to their overseas treasures. The same attention to detail was lavished on the spotless modern bathrooms. The cooking is modern and imaginative and incorporates seasonal fruits, vegetables and herbs from the enclosed kitchen garden. In another courtyard there's a medicinal herb garden with nine raised beds in Irish oak timber, each planted with herbs suitable for treating a specific part of the body. In a converted apple house, there's an aromatherapy centre offering an all-encompassing selection of massages, facials and herbal wraps. *Directions:* Take the N9 from Dublin to Royal Oak (south of Carlow), turn left into Bagenalstown (Muine Bheag), and right in the village for the 6-km drive to Kilgraney crossroads. Turn right (signposted) and Kilgraney House is the first entrance on the left (a 2-hour drive).

KILGRANEY HOUSE
Owners: Bryan Leech & Martin Marley
Bagenalstown, Co Carlow, Ireland
Tel: 059 9775283, Fax: 059 9775595
4 Rooms, Double: €130
2 Suites: €300
Dinner: €55 (not Mon or Tue)
Closed: Dec & Jan, Credit cards: all major
Country House

A stay at Echo Lodge is all about eating fabulous food in the Mustard Seed Restaurant. Head chef David Rice's four-course table d'hote menu leaves you spoilt for choice. Owner Dan Mullane is usually on hand to explain your choices in delicious detail. Much of the produce is home grown—the organic fruit and vegetable gardens are in terraces behind the hotel and the hens in the kitchen garden provide fresh free-range eggs for breakfast. The atmosphere is convivial, Dan and his staff really go the extra mile to make you welcome. Outside diners give a real buzz to the place in an evening. Bedrooms range from quirky country house to elegant suites. There's a specially designed wheelchair-friendly room. A cute little sauna and a small exercise room are also available. A Thai masseur is on hand so indulge yourself. The quiet village location is well suited for touring the southwest and playing the several surrounding golf courses. The delightful town of Adare is a 15-minute drive away and the surrounding peaceful countryside offers lots of opportunities for horse riding, fishing, clay pigeon shooting, and antique hunting. *Directions:* From Adare take the N21, Killarney road for 2 km and turn left for Ballingarry. In the village take the Newcastle West road for 500 meters and Echo Lodge is on your right.

THE MUSTARD SEED AT ECHO LODGE
Owner: Dan Mullane
Ballingarry, Co Limerick, Ireland
Tel: 069 68508, Fax: 069 68511
14 Rooms, Double: €190–€330
2 Suites: €330
Dinner: €63
Closed: first two weeks of Feb, Credit cards: all major
Ireland's Blue Book
Country House Hotel

Whitepark House has a perfect location on the prettiest part of the north Antrim coast between the famed Giant's Causeway and the precarious Carrick-a-Rede rope bridge. A narrow pathway leads down to the cluster of white cottages and tiny church that make up the much-photographed village of Portbraddan (on a sunny day one could easily imagine oneself in Greece). In clear weather views extend to Rathlin Island lighthouse and the distant Scottish islands of Islay and Jura. Small wonder that Siobhan and Bob love the area and are keen for guests to enjoy it and their home. Whitepark House was built in 1735, extended in the early 1900s and totally remodeled in 2007 to add spacious bedrooms, luxurious bathrooms and a lovely conservatory where breakfast is served overlooking the garden. Bob and Siobhan are inveterate travelers—India, Japan, Sri Lanka, Thailand, Africa. Fascinating mementos of their travels are artfully displayed alongside masses of leafy green houseplants, which flourish under Bob's tender care. Bob is happy to drive walkers to the Giant's Causeway and welcomes them home after a 13-kilometer coastal walk with homemade biscuits and tea. *Directions:* Whitepark House is on the coast road 6.5 km east of the Giant's Causeway and just over 1.5 km west of Ballintoy.

WHITEPARK HOUSE
Owners: Siobhan & Bob Isles
Ballintoy, BT45 6NH, Northern Ireland
Tel: 028 2073 1482
3 Rooms, Double: £100
Open: all year, Credit cards: MC, VS
B&B

Stella Maris has a fabulous location on the shores of Bunatrahir Bay where white topped waves cascade across the rocks and windswept sandy beaches stretch towards the rugged cliffs of Downpatrick Head. Built in 1853 as coastguard headquarters it later served as a convent. Most recently new life, as a boutique hotel, has been breathed into these sturdy buildings by Frances Kelly and Terence McSweeney. It's a stylish place with a pleasing blend of traditional and modern décor. Quite the best place to enjoy the ever-changing seascape is from the conservatory built all along the front of the building to maximize the panoramic ocean views. Dinner is cooked by Frances and enjoyed in the dining room made up of four intimate little cottage rooms—then it's back to the conservatory for coffee and drinks. Almost all of the bedrooms are ocean facing and come in queens and kings/twins all named after local and famous golf courses. The many miles of wild County Mayo coastline are yours to explore. Be sure to visit nearby Ceide Fields, an excavated Stone-Age settlement with walls older than the pyramids. *Directions:* Stella Maris is located on the ocean, 25 km west of Ballina and 2 km west of Ballycastle.

STELLA MARIS COUNTRY HOUSE HOTEL
Owners: Frances Kelly & Terry McSweeney
Ballycastle, Co. Mayo, Ireland
Tel: 096 43322, Fax: 096 43965
11 Rooms, Double: €250
Dinner: €50
Open: Easter to mid-Oct, Credit cards: MC, VS
Country House Hotel

We visited Gorman's at the insistence of Peter Haden, of Gregans Castle. We completely agree with everything he stated in his email to us: "...(This property) has a spectacular location out on the remotest part of the Dingle Peninsula overlooking Smerwick Harbour and out to the Atlantic—wild, savage scenery surrounds. The building is quite new and certainly not quaint, but the moment you step inside, there is a wonderful feeling of warmth generated by the most genuine greeting, open fires, sunny color schemes, and very comfortable furnishings. The tea and homemade biscuits make you immediately relax and feel at home. There are nine large, well-furnished bedrooms, all with fabulous views and good bathrooms with buckets of hot water and all the little extras. The dining room is designed to take advantage of the views, and we had dinner watching the sun set on the Atlantic horizon. Food is fine without being famous, and service is very friendly. Rarely before have I stayed in a place where I had such a good feeling of genuine friendliness and warmth from the owners, who are dedicated to providing the best for everyone. What more can I say?" Only that the food is excellent. *Directions:* Go through Dingle town keeping the harbor on your left. At the roundabout west of town, go straight (signpost An Fheothanach)—Gorman's is 13 km on. After about 8 km the road forks: stay left and you come back to the coast—the sea is on your right and Gorman's is on your left.

GORMAN'S CLIFFTOP HOUSE
Owners: Sile & Vincent Gorman
Glaise Bheag
(Baile na nGall) Dingle Peninsula
Ballydavid, Co. Kerry, Ireland
Tel: 066 915 162, Fax: 066 9155 162
9 Rooms, Double: €130–€170
Dinner: €40 (not Sun)
Closed: Christmas, Credit cards: MC, VS
Guesthouse

This tall, bright-white Victorian house set amidst lush gardens rimming the shores of Bantry Bay is a most hospitable welcoming hotel. Run by Kathleen O'Sullivan and her gracious long time staff the atmosphere is friendly and informal, which accounts, I am sure, for the large number of guests who return here year after year. Enjoy a pre-dinner drink in the sitting room bar and select your dinner from the tempting menu which usually includes fresh seafood—we particularly enjoyed out selections of locally raised duck and fresh lemon sole. For those in search of peace and quiet there is an old-fashioned parlor/TV room. The dining room is cleverly divided into several areas which creates a most enjoyable experience. Be sure to request a room at the front of the house for a great many these rooms have tempting glimpses of the bay across the gardens and through the trees. Two garden view rooms have been especially equipped for the handicapped. The scenery hereabouts is absolutetely spectacular. If you have time, wander off the main roads to explore the Beara Peninsula with its views of barren, rocky mountains tumbling into the sea. A "must visit" is nearby Garinish Island, a spectacular garden with trees, shrubs, and plants from every part of the world. Just down the road is Bantry House, a grand mansion that is well worth a visit. *Directions:* Seaview House Hotel is located in Ballylickey on the N71 between Bantry and Glengarriff.

🍺 ✒ 💳 ☎ 🐕 @ W P ⑪ 🏞 ♿ 🚶 👫 🐎 ⚓

SEAVIEW HOUSE HOTEL
Owner: Kathleen O'Sullivan
Ballylickey, Co Cork, Ireland
Tel: 027 50073, Fax: 027 51555
25 Rooms, Double: €80–€100
6 Suites: €200
Dinner: €55
Open: mid-Mar to mid-Nov, Credit cards: all major
Country House Hotel

Olive and Paddy O'Gorman have a relaxed, easygoing attitude to life. They welcome guests to the wing of their commodious farmhouse nestled in the pretty Nire Valley, an area of Ireland off the beaten tourist path and noted for its beautiful scenery. Knowing that you deserve the best, request one of Olive's premier rooms with Jacuzzi tub and shower. Olive takes great pride in her bedrooms not only matching the bedspread and drapes with the wallpaper but taking it so far to see that each room has cups and saucers that match the room's colorful decor. Olive finds it no problem at all to juggle her family and a houseful of guests, chatting with them over tea and cake when they arrive, feeding them copious breakfasts, packing tempting lunches, arranging for them to go walking and feeding them dinner in the conservatory on their return. Guests come to this quiet corner of County Waterford to walk the Comeragh Mountains and experience Irish farmhouse hospitality. If the outdoor pursuits of fishing, pony-trekking, and walking are not your cup of tea, you can drive to Lismore, Cashel, or over The Vee, returning in time for a visit to one of the nearby pubs for a late-night Irish music session. *Directions:* From Clonmel or Dungarven follow the R671 to Ballymacarbry. Glasha is signposted to your right just before you reach Ballymacarbry if you are coming from Clonmel or just after to your left if you are coming from Dungarven.

GLASHA
Owners: Olive & Paddy O'Gorman
Via Clonmel
Ballymacarbry, Co. Waterford, Ireland
Tel & Fax: 052 36108
8 Rooms, Double: €100–€120
Dinner: €25–€45 (not Sun)
Closed: Christmas, Credit cards: MC, VS
Farmhouse B&B

Marlagh Lodge dates back to 1853. It was originally built for Henry Hutchinson Hamilton O'Hara, son of local landholders and residents of nearby Crebilly Castle. Now a listed building it is described as an interesting Victorian mix of picturesque and Georgian elements, gabled bays and roof overhangs. Standing in its own grounds adjacent to the A3 secondary glazing helps to keep the high ceilinged bedrooms warm and reduces traffic noise to a minimum. Current owners Robert and Rachel Thompson have brought the property back to its former glory with the careful eye of experienced practitioners, a four poster here, a brass bed there, antiques and collectibles, black iron and tile fireplaces. The piano in the study attests to the Thompsons' musical talents. A hearty breakfast is served in the dining room, home made bread, local produce, porridge or a traditional Ulster Fry. A twenty minute drive finds you at Belfast International airport. Marlagh Lodge is ideal for visiting Belfast but the great draw lies in the opposite directions where you find the Giants Causeway and the lovely Antrim coast. *Directions:* Exit the M2 at Antrim and take the A26 to Ballymena. At the first roundabout take the A36 Larne and at the second the A36 Larne. After 1km you see the house on the right, turn right into Rankinstown Road and immediate left into the driveway.

MARLAGH LODGE
Owners: Rachel & Robert Thompson
71 Moorfields Road
Ballymena, BT42 3BU, Northern Ireland
Tel: 028 2563 1505, Fax: 028 2564 1590
3 Rooms, Double: £90
Dinner: £32.50
Closed: Christmas & New Year, Credit cards: MC, VS
Hidden Ireland
Country House

When I travel I'm always in search of something that is completely different from home and this is the case here as most of my house would fit itnot the entrance hall where Roderick and Helena Perceval keep the "wellies", fishing paraphernalia, and inclement weather gear. And that's just the tip of the iceberg for beyond lie rooms of enormous proportions. One bedroom is aptly named the half acre. Another is the twins' room because it has two of everything—all pleasingly idiosyncratic and just bursting with character. Furniture made for the house is still here along with a grand array of family portraits. Roderick makes certain guests are introduced to one another when they gather fro pre-dinner drinks round the fire in the snug little sitting room. Whenever I have stayed there have always been the most interesting of dinner conversations with my fellow guests around the polished dining room table and, of course, the food is always excellent. As for what to do during the day—some folks never leave the estate: there's a vast lake for fishing (a boat is available for pike fishing), a lakeside castle built by the Knights Templar in 1200, a huge walled garden, and miles of walking paths (Roderick will give you a map). The Percevals have lived here since 1665 and there are some wonderful stories of ancestors' exploits. *Directions:* From Sligo take the N4 to the N17 (Galway road). The house is signpost to the left 0.5km south of Ballinacarrow.

TEMPLE HOUSE
Owners: Helena & Roderick Perceval
Ballinacarrow
Ballymote, Co. Sligo, Ireland
Tel: 071 9183329, Fax: 071 9183808
6 Rooms, Double: €160–€190
2 Cottages: €350–€995 weekly
Dinner: €47– €50 (not Sun)
Open: Apr to Nov, Credit cards: MC, VS
Hidden Ireland
Country House & Self Catering

Ballinkeele House offers guests peace and tranquillity and the opportunity to enjoy accommodation and hospitality of a gentler age. Built in 1840 for the Maher family, the house has all the solid quality of a grand home with large rooms, fine ceilings and decorative doors. Oriental rugs dress the flagstone entry, which is warmed by a huge, old fashioned stove, and grand oil paintings and family portraits adorn the walls. Antique furniture graces the cosy drawing room and enormous dining room where guests enjoy delicious candlelight dinners. The Master Bedroom is a particularly large room decorated in soft red and beiges with an impressive four-poster bed sitting center stage. Central heating and modern bathrooms add to the comfort of the large bedrooms. For recreation, there are walks through the estate, bicycles available and croquet on the lawn. Settle in for several nights and enjoy County Wexfords new theatre, (home to the Wexford Festival Opera), Irish National Heritage Park, Kennedy Homestead or go for a walk on Curracloe Beach (used for the filming of Saving Private Ryan). Within just over an hour's drive, are the ancient city of Kilkenny (with its splendid castle) and Waterford city (renowned for the Crystal factory). *Directions:* From Dublin take the N11, Wexford road, to Gorey. Turn left at the traffic lights for Wexford (R741) for 30 km and the 5-km drive to Ballinkeele House is signposted on your right.

BALLINKEELE HOUSE
Owners: Margaret & John Maher
Ballymurn
Enniscorthy, Co. Wexford, Ireland
Tel: 053 9138105, Fax: 053 9138468
5 Rooms, Double: €150–€190
Dinner: €45 (not Tue)
Open: Feb to Nov, Credit cards: all major
Hidden Ireland
Country House

Ballynahinch Castle, former home of the O'Flaherty chieftains, a pirate queen and a maharajah, has enjoyed a long and colorful history. The heart of this friendly hotel is the bar with its old brick floor and little tables surrounded by Windsor chairs. Here a long table displays the "catch of the day" and fisherfolk hang the keys that give them access to the little huts on their fishing beats—no need to stand out in the rain when fishing here. The beats are so close to the house that folks return to the bar for lunch (packed lunches are also available). Bar food is served in the evening for those who are not inclined to partake of a more formal meal in the dining room whose windows overlook the river. Bedrooms come in three varieties: standard, superior, and luxury, which at Ballynahinch Castle means large, larger, and largest. On a recent visit I was particularly impressed by rooms on the top floor with their lovely décor and top of the line bathrooms. Plans are moving ahead to add an all things outdoors store to the courtyard along with a workout room and the opportunity to enjoy a massage. The beauty of Connemara is on your doorstep, Helpful staff assist you in planning daytrips. Often guests never leave the hotel's property, spending their days wandering through the 450 acres of grounds or by the fire with a book. *Directions:* From Galway take the N59 Clifden for 68 km and turn left for Roundstone. The hotel is on your right after 4 km.

BALLYNAHINCH CASTLE
Manager: Patrick O'Flaherty
Ballynahinch
Connemara, Co. Galway, Ireland
Tel: 095 31006, Fax: 095 31085
40 Rooms, Double: €220–€420*
*Service: 10%
Dinner: €55
Closed: Feb, Credit cards: all major
Country House Hotel

With The Burren sheltering its back and a panoramic view of Ballyvaughan Bay to the towering cliffs of Black Head in front, Drumcreehy House commands an location just outside the picturesque village of Ballyvaughan. Bernadette and Armin designed this house to look as old as possible while including all modern amenities. To add to the traditional feel, they have furnished the sitting room and dining room with antiques, and all the bedrooms with old pine. Spring Gentian and Dog Violet are especially spacious with larger shower rooms, and along with Cowslip and Primrose enjoy spectacular views across the bay to Black Head. If you are not up to stairs request a room in the adjacent two bedroom cottage—perfect for families. Coffee, tea and an honesty bar are available in a cozy little room off the sitting room. Enjoy a cooked breakfast in the sunny yellow breakfast room where a vast sidebarard laden with fruit, cereal, cheeses, smoked salmon and meats caused me to cancel my cooked breakfast. Shannon is an hour's drive away, making this an ideal first or last night on your trip, but stay longer and explore the beautiful Burren and beyond. *Directions:* From Shannon take the N18 to Ennis, the N85 towards Ennistymon, and the first right through Corofin and on towards Kilfenora. At the ruined castle turn right for Ballyvaughan and go about 10 km to the village. At Hylands Hotel, turn right and the house is on the righ after 1 km.

DRUMCREEHY HOUSE
Owners: Bernadette & Armin Grefkes
Ballyvaughan, Co Clare, Ireland
Tel: 065 7077377, Fax: 065 7077379
10 Rooms, Double: €80–€120
Open: all year, Credit cards: MC, VS
Guesthouse

Gregans Castle is only 57 kilometers from Shannon airport, so if you are heading north or west, this is the perfect spot to begin your stay in Ireland. This is not an imposing castle, but a sprawling manor house set in lovely gardens in a lush green valley completely surrounded by The Burren, with its "moonscapes" of gray limestone and scattered alpine and arctic plants. While there are several comfortable lounges to congregate in, my preference is the beamed Corkscrew bar with its blazing turf fire. Lunch is served here, and in the evening guests gather for a drink and a chat. From the dining room, where tables are reserved for all guests for dinner each night, windows frame outstanding views of The Burren sweeping down to the edge of Galway Bay. On a recent visit I really liked Gleninagh—a standard twin room with a particularly nice bathroom, Mina's room—a superior king-bedded room in the oldest part of the house facing Galway Bay, and the three garden suites with their private patios and brand new bathrooms. Local attractions include the Ailwee Caves, full of stalactites and stalagmites, and the Cliffs of Moher. *Directions:* From Shannon take the N18 to Ennis, the N85 towards Ennistymon, the first right (R476) through Corofin, and on towards Kilfenora. At the ruined castle turn right onto the R480 towards Ballyvaughan and, as you crest The Burren, you see the hotel in the valley below.

GREGANS CASTLE
Owners: Simon Haden & Frederieke McMurray
Ballyvaughan, Co. Cork, Ireland
Tel: 065 7077005, Fax: 065 7077111
15 Rooms, Double: €195–€235
6 Suites: €295–€450
Dinner: €35–€60
Open: Feb 14 to Nov 30, Credit cards: all major
Ireland's Blue Book
Country House Hotel

Dating back to 1750 this stately home sits in an elevated position with magnificent views across Bantry Bay. The current owner, descendant of the Earls of Bantry, Egerton Shelswell-White opens the house and gardens to the public who, with information sheets in hand, tour its lofty rooms and admire its elegant furniture, tapestries and paintings, retiring afterwards to the tearoom in the old refectory. Yet this is a stately home with a difference for one entire wing of the house has been renovated to provide six large airy guestrooms, each with a top of the line bathroom. I was particularly impressed with room 25, its curving wall of windows and window seats overlooking the bay. Breakfast is prepared for you in the smartly decorated dining room in what used to be one of the old cellars. At night toast your toes by the fire in the little lounge, help yourself to drinks from the honesty bar, play billiards in the enormous billiard room or, if you wish, slip through the concealed door into the long gallery to wander at leisure through the museum like rooms of this grand old home. In addition two spacious, more simply decorated, family rooms are found above the tearoom. Dinner can be arranged for parties that rent the entire wing. There are several restaurants that you can walk to in town. *Directions:* Bantry is on the N71 between Skibereen and Kenmare. Turn through the arched gatehouse (beside the large white hotel on the waterfront) and drive up to the house.

BANTRY HOUSE
Owners: Brigitte & Egerton Shelswell-White
Bantry, Co. Cork, Ireland
Tel: 027 50047, Fax: 027 50795
8 Rooms, Double: €180–€300
1 Cottage: €450–€750 weekly
Dinner: €35
Open: mid-Mar to Nov, Credit cards: MC, VS
Hidden Ireland
Country House & Self Catering

Rosemary and Brian McAuley had Dunauley designed to take advantage of the spectacular view of the island-dotted Bantry Bay, aptly framed be a wall of windows in the living/dining room. Three double-bedded bedrooms, each with a simple en suite shower room are found on the same level as the living room. Downstairs is an additional bedroom with a magnificent view. A snug one bedroom apartment (queen plus single bed) has its own entrance and can be rented on a weekly basis. Guests enjoy the living room and its particularly fine view as they sit round the fire in an evening and while tucking into an ample breakfast before setting out on a days sightseeing. The drive from Bantry to Glengarriff gives a taste of the rugged landscape and exotic flora that you find in this part of Ireland. From Glengarriff you can take a boat to Garinish Island, a lush collection of shrubs, trees and flowers from all over the world. For over three years over one hundred men worked to make Arran Bryce's garden, caseta and temple; but financial hardships precluded the building of his home. *Directions:* From the center of Bantry follow white signs for the hospital through the one-way system and up the hill. Pass a church on the right and continue on this road till you see Dunauley signposted to the right—keep going uphill to the house.

DUNAULEY
Owners: Rosemary & Brian McAuley
Seskin
Bantry, Co Cork, Ireland
Tel & Fax: 027 50290
4 Rooms, Double: €80–€90
1 Apartment: €350–€450 weekly
Open: May to Sep, Credit cards: none
B&B & Self Catering

Ash-Rowan is the relaxed, very friendly, unpretentious home of Sam and Evelyn Hazlett—an excellent choice for a bed and breakfast while staying in the northern capital. A varied choice of breakfasts sets you up for the day—opt for organic porridge flavored with Drambuie and cream served with pancakes; Irish scramble with eggs, chopped bacon, and mushrooms, or the Ulster Fry, the ultimate cooked breakfast which the menu warns is not for the faint hearted. Vegetarians should try the flambéed mushrooms or vegetarian omlette. It's a climb to the top of the house (no large cases!) but worth it to secure one of the choice rooms (7 and 8) that offer more spacious quarters. All the rooms have TVs, phones, bathrobes, and hospitality trays with biscuits, teas, coffee, and instant soups. Beds are made with crisply starched linen sheets and pillowcases. The location, near the university, is perfect for strolling into the city and taxis are inexpensive for a night out on the town. Peruse the papers and the tourist literature in the wonderfully cluttered conservatory then seek out Sam or Evelyn to set you up with sightseeing venues for the day. *Directions:* From central Belfast take Dublin Road to Shaftesbury Square. Go through Bradbury Place onto University Road. Pass Queen's University on the left and go straight through the traffic lights into Malone Road. Windsor Avenue is the fifth avenue on your right.

ASH-ROWAN
Owners: Evelyn & Sam Hazlett
12 Windsor Avenue
Belfast, BT9 6EE, Northern Ireland
Tel: 028 9066 1758, Fax: 028 9066 3227
5 Rooms, Double: £96–£110
Closed: Christmas & New Year, Credit cards: MC, VS
Guesthouse

This impressive building with its façade of carved stonework columns and statuary dates back to 1860. Originally constructed as the grand headquarters of the Ulster Bank, it has been extensively remodeled and renovated prior to opening as a five-star hotel. Guestrooms feature dramatically high ceilings, custom furniture, antiques, original artwork and sumptuous soft furnishings. Splendid en-suite bathrooms with brown marble, white porcelain, sparkling chrome and glass are no less than would be expected. All the electronic needs of today's traveler, large flat-screen TV's, wireless internet and CD/DVD players complete the picture. Suites, with their splendid hip-bath soaking tubs, are located in the original bank management living quarters. Vaults, with their massive steel doors intact, have been converted to wine cellars and a snooker room. "The Bar", which specializes in cocktails, is to be found adjacent to the appropriately named "Great Room" Restaurant. The latter, created in what was the original public banking area is the epitome of elegance. The Restaurant, which features intricate plasterwork, an antique Clevi harp, a huge Tyrone Crystal chandelier, discreetly separated tables and rich décor, serves breakfast, lunch and dinner, and afternoon teas. *Directions:* From the M3 , take the A2 South, turn left at Ann Street, turn right at Victoria Street and left at Waring St. to the hotel. Double park to unload and you will be directed to nearby parking.

THE MERCHANT HOTEL
Owner: Bill Wolsey
Manager: Adrian Mclaughlan
35-39 Waring Street
Belfast, BT1 2DY, Northern Ireland
Tel: 028 9023 4888, Fax: 028 9024 7775
26 Rooms, Double: £240–£640
Open: all year, Credit cards: all major
Ireland's Blue Book
City Hotel

Set just across the street from Belfast's historic City Hall, Ten Square is a contemporary up-market town house hotel, built on the site of the old Post Office. A welcoming fire warms the seating area in the reception hall. On the ground floor the bustling public bar with its wooden columns, brick faced walls, leather cushioned seats and raffia lanterns is a lively meeting place for young and old alike. The equally stylish adjacent Grill Room restaurant with its leather benches, hardback chairs, dark wooden floors and tables, sparkling glass and silverware serves a typical bistro style menu supported by a very reasonably priced international wine list. Stylish bedrooms are to be found on the two floors above; pale earthtones are offset with splashed of color. Furnishings border on minimalist, but the work of local artist Terry Bradley is prominently displayed. King sized beds, high ceilings, all modern electronic conveniences and sparkling black and white tile bathrooms complete the picture. Ten Square is handy for walking to everything in central Belfast. *Directions:* Arriving in Belfast take the M2 and follow signs for city centre. Take the 1st right and 1st left in front and beside City Hall and you find Ten Square behind city hall on the corner of Linen Hall Street. Park in front to unload and be directed to an overnight stay car park.

TEN SQUARE
Owners: Nicholas & Paul Hill
10 Donegal Square South
Belfast, BT1 5JD, Northern Ireland
Tel: 028 9024 1001, Fax: 028 9024 3210
22 Rooms, Double: £170–£220
1 Suite: £265
Open: all year, Credit cards: all major
City Hotel

John and Ann are particularly gregarious hosts, perhaps influenced by their close proximity to the Blarney stone, said to confer the "gift of the gab." John would have you believe that you can tour the entire south of Ireland from their guesthouse. While this is somewhat of an exaggeration, it certainly is an ideal base for visiting Cork, Cobh, Kinsale, as well as enjoying a day in Blarney where the castle's lovely grounds and Blarney woolen mills are great attractions. While Ashlee Lodge may seem unremarkable from the road, the place is full of surprises. Comfortable bedrooms can all be either twin or king, with large TVs and CD players. They come in three sizes: executive—good size rooms with shower over the tub, garden—larger rooms with Jacuzzi bathtubs, or master—very large rooms with sitting area and Jacuzzi bathtubs. One bedroom is totally wheelchair friendly. There's also an upstairs deck with a hot tub. Drinks are served from the honesty bar in the evening and the light and airy breakfast room (lots of choices as well as a cooked Irish breakfast) doubles as the restaurant in the evening. Golf is endemic hereabouts and John will gladly arrange tee times and transportation. If you want to travel without a car, airport pickup can be arranged. Handily the bus to Blarney and Cork runs by the front door. *Directions:* Ashlee Lodge is located in Tower, 2 km west of Blarney. The house is on the R617—the Blarney to Killarney Road.

❄ 🍵 ⚗ 💳 ☎ 🏠 @ W P 🍴 🚭 ❀ 🖼 ♿ ⛵ 🕺 ⛷

ASHLEE LODGE
Owners: Anne & John O'Leary
Blarney, Co. Cork, Ireland
Tel: 021 4385346, Fax: 021 4385726
10 Rooms, Double: €99–€140
2 Suites: €160–€250
Dinner: €40 (not Sun or Mon)
Closed: Christmas & New Year, Credit cards: MC, VS
Guesthouse

Bobbie Smith's home reflects her welcoming, easygoing personality. Filled with mellow old furniture, books, pictures, and family mementos, the Old Rectory is very much a lived-in, comfortable family home for Bobbie and her three daughters. Guests are welcomed with a reviving pot of tea in the homey drawing room, and it is here that they chat with fellow guests before dinner, which is taken by candlelight round the long, gleaming dining room table. Bedrooms have the same traditional family feel and range from a snug twin to two spacious rooms, one with a carved four-poster and the other with a splendid Victorian bed with turned posts decorating the foot and headboard. All have en suite shower rooms and there's an extra "bath" so that those who love to soak can do so in a claw-foot tub. The area is perfect for cycling; and holidays that include cycle hire, airport pickup, and baggage transportation can be arranged. Those who prefer to stick to their car will find Kilkenny with its castle, fine old shops, and lovely buildings just a 20-minute drive away. Day trips can be taken to Wexford, Kildare, and Glendalough. *Directions:* Take the N9 from Dublin to Royal Oak (south of Carlow), turn left into Bagenalstown, and right in the village for the 6-km drive to Lorum Old Rectory.

LORUM OLD RECTORY
Owner: Bobbie Smith
Kilgreaney, Bagenalstown
Borris, Co. Carlow, Ireland
Tel: 059 9775282, Fax: 059 9775455
5 Rooms, Double: €150–€160
Dinner: €45
Closed: Nov to Feb, Credit cards: MC, VS
Hidden Ireland
Country House

Bruckless House was built in the mid-18th century and lived in by the Cassidy brothers, traders and merchants who sold guns to Napoleon and pickled herrings to Wellington in Portugal. Later the house was owned by a passionate Communist, Commander Fforde, who is remembered for his many good works in the area. Continuing the tradition of colorful owners, Clive and Joan Evans moved here after spending many years in Hong Kong. This lovely home has the most marvelous location, set in wooded acres with garden paths leading down to the rocky shoreline of Bruckless Bay. Colorful Oriental rugs warm the flagstone entryway and mementos of the Evans' years abroad blend with comfortable family antiques. A log fire warms the dining room on chilly mornings as guests breakfast together round the long polished table. Bedrooms are found in what was once the children's wing up the back staircase. Nanny's Room is a delightful twin-bedded room with an en suite bathroom with a power shower over the tub, and a double-bedded room also has an en suite bathroom. Both rooms have single rooms adjacent to them for children. At the top of the driveway, an adorable two-bedroom lodge is perfect for families who wish to stay for several days (in summer it is let on a weekly basis). Bruckless is ideally placed for exploring Donegal. *Directions:* From Donegal take the N56 towards Killybegs. The house is on the left in Bruckless village.

BRUCKLESS HOUSE
Owners: Joan & Clive Evans
Bruckless, Co Donegal, Ireland
Tel: 074 9737071, Fax: 074 9737070
4 Rooms, Double: €110–€130
1 Cottage: €230–€500 weekly
Open: Apr to Sep, Credit cards: all major
Country House & Self Catering

This onetime coaching inn was in a sad and sorry state before it was rescued by the present owner, Roy Bolton, and transformed into the delightful hotel you see today. A rocking chair sits before an enormous fireplace and displays of old plates adorn the mantle. The ambiance of an old coaching inn continues to the restaurant with its whitewashed stone walls and tall pine settles dividing the room into intimate little areas. The inn's original kitchen, with its flagstone floor and open fire, links the hotel to the Victorian-style bar still illuminated by flickering gas light. Try a Black Bush whiskey from the distillery up the road—Bushmills is the home of the world's oldest licensed distillery and you can take a tour around it. There is a broad range of bedrooms. The most desirable are definitely the Superior Rooms of the Mill House, where you can expect to be pampered up to best 5-star standards. However, all the Mill House rooms are spacious with a small sitting area and ample room for luggage and golf clubs (lots of excellent courses nearby, including Royal Portrush). Small budget price rooms are also available in the original Coaching Inn overlooking the village. Just up the road are the picturesque ruins of 13th-century Dunluce Castle and the Giant's Causeway. *Directions:* From Coleraine take the B19 to Bushmills. As you cross the River Bush, the main entrance to the hotel is on your left.

BUSHMILLS INN HOTEL
Manager: Alan Dunlop
9 Dunluce Road
Bushmills, BT57 8QG, Northern Ireland
Tel: 028 2073 3000, Fax: 028 2073 2048
32 Rooms, Double: £98–£268
Dinner: from £30
Open: all year, Credit cards: MC, VS
Ireland's Blue Book
Inn

Just four kilometers from the Ring of Kerry, Iskeroon is one of the most secluded properties in Ireland, reached by a precipitous lane that tumbles down to the sea and a narrow farm track. Geraldine and David, an easy-going couple with two young children are the first family to call this home. The property was built in the '30s by the Earl of Dunraven, and used as holiday home. Snuggling into a sheltered spot guests enjoy two suites and a self-catering apartment in the wisteria-clad coach house adjacent to the main house. The accommodations have wireless broadband, cable TV and well equipped kitchens, lots of interesting books, games and IPod docking stations. They are available for both B&B (minimum two nights) or self catering (minimum 4 nights). Guests enjoy splendid sea views from the garden and the private pier. The nearby town of Waterville has a good selection of restaurants for dinner. A not to be missed boat trip runs from Bunavalla pier to the Skellig Islands. Drives through splendid Ring of Kerry and Killarney scenery are a must. Derrynane is between Waterville and Caherdaniel. *Directions:* Find the Scarriff Inn (a large red building) between these villages and take the road signposted Bunavalla Pier all the way to the bottom. At the pier turn left over the track beside the beach to Iskeroon.

ISKEROON
Owners: Geraldine & David Hare
Caherdaniel
Derrynane, Co. Kerry, Ireland
Tel: 066 9475119, Fax: 066 9475488
2 Suites: €175 daily, €600 weekly
1 Apartment: €550 weekly
Open: May to Sep, Credit cards: all major
B&B & Self Catering

Ballaghtobin has everything: a beautifully decorated and furnished interior; acres of scenic parkland with a ruined Norman church just steps from the front door; an excellent location for exploring the Counties of Waterford and Kilkenny; and the most welcoming of owners in Mickey and Catherine Gabbett. Catherine's flair for interior design is evident in every elegant, informal room—soft, warm pastel walls, beautiful paintings, lovely antiques—it's very easy to settle in here. Bedrooms are absolutely gorgeous and have sparkling modern bathrooms. My favorite is the spacious Barrack Room—in years gone by, guests who drank too much at parties were sent here to sleep. Breakfast is the only meal served and for dinner guests often go to the Hunter Yard at Mount Juliet. You could really spend a week doing something totally different each day. There is medieval Kilkenny city with its wealth of historical sights; the craft trail that combines potters, leather makers, and glass blowers; golf courses from local to championship; Waterford with its historic harbor and famous crystal; and Cashel with its rock and historic abbey. *Directions:* From the main crossroads in the center of Callan take the road signed "Callan Garden Centre" (Mill Street). Go straight for 5 km (past Callan golf Club) and follow a sharp bend to the left. Take the left fork at the Y-junction (house is signposted) and after about .5 km Ballaghtobin's entrance is on your left opposite a pink gate lodge.

BALLAGHTOBIN
Owners: Catherine & Mickey Gabbett
Callan, Co Kilkenny, Ireland
Tel: 056 7725227, Fax: 056 7725712
3 Rooms, Double: €100
Closed: Dec & Jan, Credit cards: MC, VS
Country House

This is the place to stay if you are a garden buff for this lovely Georgian house, built in 1794, is surrounded by 7 acres of glorious gardens. Started in 1947, the gardens extend from walled formality with trim lawns and herbaceous borders to a magical informal woodland garden complete with millpond and literary corner where you can curl up with a good book. It's home to Mark and Emma Hewlett and their three young boys who Emma fervently hopes will be keen gardeners too. It's a lovely place to base yourself for explorations along the southeast coast. An ideal place to relax and enjoy the spectacular gardens, tennis court, heated indoor pool, exercise room or indulge yourself with a massage and aromatherapy session. Dinner in the peacock dining room is a real treat there's always fresh fish on the menu and most of the vegetables and fruit comes from the extensive kitchen garden. Breakfast and lunch are enjoyed in the airy conservatory which doubles as the Pink Teacup café for daytime garden visitors. Two interconnecting courtyard bedrooms are especially handy for families and friends traveling together. In the house Magnolia is an particularly inviting room with its large four-poster bed and clawfoot-tub with garden view. The Coach House and the Garden Suite are two lovely, self-catering apartments. *Directions:* From New Ross take the R733 signposted Campile and follow signposts to Kilmokea Gardens.

KILMOKEA   ***Cover painting***
Owners: Emma & Mark Hewlett
Campile
Great Island, Co. Wexford, Ireland
Tel: 051 388109, Fax: 051 388766
6 Rooms, Double: €180–€300
2 Apartments: €750–€1250 weekly
Dinner: €50
Open: Feb to Oct, Credit cards: MC, VS
Hidden Ireland
Country House Hotel & Self Catering

Paul's parents bought this huge home when he was a child and quickly discovered that it was far too large to maintain as a family home without an army of staff, so they opened it up to guests. His mum, Jean, while claiming to be retired still enthusiastically advises guests on where to go and what to see between breakfast and dinner—she has enough sightseeing venues to occupy a fortnight. Wife Clare does the front of house in an evening while Paul is in the kitchen. Up the grand staircase there are some very spacious, well equipped and comfortable bedrooms—be sure to discuss the size of bed, several are large zip-and-link beds while others are smaller with lovely old head and footboards. Do not miss the opportunity to visit Lismore Castle, Swiss Cottage, and Waterford Crystal, or to take a drive over The Vee. You need to keep busy to work off the delicious dinners that Paul prepares (a set four-course menu with choices or the flexibility of being able to order à la carte). Old and new guests alike revel in the relaxed idiosyncrasy of the place. *Directions:* From Waterford take the N72 (Killarney road) for about a one-hour drive to Cappoquin. Richmond House is on the left just before you enter town.

RICHMOND HOUSE
Owner: The Deevy family
Cappoquin, Co Waterford, Ireland
Tel: 058 54278, Fax: 058 54988
9 Rooms, Double: €160–€250
Dinner: €55 (not Sun)
Open: Feb to Dec, Credit cards: all major
Country House Hotel

Hollywell is set in a large garden overlooking the River Shannon. It has a secluded riverside location, just a couple of minutes' walk to the heart of Carrick-on-Shannon, a lively riverside town. Tom and Rosaleen provide outstanding hospitality in their lovely old home. Guests have a large sitting room with comfy sofas, books, games, and TV where they gather round the fire in the evening. Breakfast is the only meal served at the little tables arranged round the grand piano in the dining room, but for dinner guests often go to the Oarsman on Bridge Street run by sons Conor and Ronan. Three grandfather clocks grace the hallways and a sofa and books are grouped at the head of the stairs to take advantage of the view over a broad stretch of the river. The two very large front bedrooms share the same lovely view, while the back bedrooms are small only in comparison to those at the front. You can fish without ever leaving Hollywell's grounds and there's an 18-hole golf club nearby. A few of the stately houses within reach are Strokestown House and Gardens, Clonalis, King House, Florence Court, Castle Coole, and Belvedere House and Gardens. Ask about the possibility of renting a launch for a day and take a little meander up the River Shannon. *Directions:* From Dublin take the N4 (Sligo road) to Carrick. Cross the river, turn up the hill by Gings pub, and Hollywell is on the left.

HOLLYWELL
Owners: Rosaleen & Tom Maher
Liberty Hill
Carrick-on-Shannon, Co. Leitrim, Ireland
Tel & Fax: 071 9621124
4 Rooms, Double: €110–€140
Closed: Nov to Mar, Credit cards: all major
Country House

The setting for Cashel House is spectacular: at the head of Cashel Bay with Cashel Hill standing guard behind, a solid white house nestles amongst acres and acres of woodland and gardens of exotic flowering shrubs. Kilometers of garden footpaths are yours to wander along, and the beautiful seashore is yours to explore. This is not the kind of hotel to spend just a night in—once you have settled into your lovely room and sampled the exquisite food in the splendid conservatory dining room, you will be glad that you have made Cashel House the base for your Connemara explorations. Graceful antiques, turf fires, and lovely arrangements of freshly picked flowers create a warm, country-house welcome. It feels particularly decadent to have breakfast served to you in bed on a prettily decorated tray. All the bedrooms are beautifully furnished and decorated, each accompanied by a sparkling bathroom. Thirteen exquisite suites occupy a wing and enjoy comfortable sitting areas overlooking the garden. Keen tennis players can enjoy the court bordering the bay. Be sure to visit the horses in the stables behind the hotel. The McEvillys can arrange for a car and driver to meet you at Galway airport. Day trips with a car and driver can also be arranged. Just down the road a small two bedroom cottage, with bay views, is let on a weekly basis. *Directions:* Take the N59 from Galway (towards Clifden) through Oughterard and turn left to the village of Cashel 2 km after Recess.

CASHEL HOUSE
Owners: Kay & Dermot McEvilly
Cashel, Co. Galway, Ireland
Tel: 095 31001, Fax: 095 31077
19 Rooms, Double: €190–€350*
13 Suites: €270–€350*
*Service: 12.5%
Dinner: €60
Closed: mid-Jan to mid-Feb, Credit cards: all major
Relais & Châteaux
Country House Hotel & Self Catering

Cashel Palace was built as the Bishop of Cashel's sumptuous home in 1730. The bishop chose a prime location with an unparalleled view of the Rock of Cashel, which rises above the town topped by the ruins of a 13th-century cathedral. A grand staircase leads to the second-floor bedrooms where a lavish array of accommodation awaits. The grand Bishop's Bedroom (room 15) and room 11 with its grand four-poster bed and luxurious bathroom with tub and shower stand out as particular favorites. On the third floor, rooms are smaller with windows that peek out over the town or the gardens. An additional ten bedrooms are found in the adjacent mews house. The Bishop's Buttery, in the old vaulted palace cellars, offers the opportunity for fine dining. Casual by contrast, the adjacent bar reigns as the true "home" of Guinness, for it was first brewed here in 1740. The friendly staff are particularly helpful. Right in the town's center, the palace marks the perfect spot for browsing through the shops. Allow time to wander around the gardens, where the mulberry tree on the lawn was planted in 1702. Through the gate to the Bishop's Walk lies a private path that zigzags up the Rock of Cashel. *Directions:* If you are looking for the ocean and Connemara this is the wrong Cashel! Cashel is northeast of Cork on the N8, Dublin road. Find the tourist office, in the centre of town, and the entrance to Cashel Palace is adjacent to it, next to the large cross.

CASHEL PALACE
Owners: Susan & Patrick Murphy
Main Street
Cashel, Co. Tipperary, Ireland
Tel: 062 62707, Fax: 062 61521
23 Rooms, Double: €185–€370
Dinner: €55
Open: all year, Credit cards: all major
Ireland's Blue Book
Country House Hotel

Ballyvolane is a great Irish country house. Set a few miles from Fermoy it's a perfect place for sightseeing between Waterford and Kinsale, Cashel to Lismore. It is beautiful at night when the long mahogany table is set with flickering candles and you enjoy drinks by the fire in the grand pillared hallway. It is lovely on a warm morning as you wander through the gardens. It's one of those houses that makes you feel happy just thinking about having stayed there. It's a friendly house where guests make themselves thoroughly at home. It is welcoming because Justin and Jenny Green suffuse it with their young energy, their charm and friendliness. Bedrooms in the house are roomy, stylish and furnished with antiques. One has a bath so deep that you have to step up to get into it. Want something different and totally private? Opt for one of the five cottages in the walled garden whose bedrooms, complete with sunken tub, overlooks the garden while the living room windows peer over the garden wall. Within a radius of a few kilometers there are 20 golf courses and within an hour's drive are Blarney with its famous castle, Cork city, and the bustling boating town of Kinsale. Ballyvolane has seven kilometers of privately managed salmon fishing on the renowned River Blackwater. A self-catering cottage is also available. *Directions:* From Fermoy take the N8 towards Cork to Rathcormac, and Ballyvolane House is 6 km further on down a signposted country lane.

■ ≈ CREDIT ▲ P ⅙ ⊥ ⅂ ♐ ⅄

BALLYVOLANE HOUSE
Owners: Jenny & Justin Green
Castlelyons, Co Cork, Ireland
Tel: 025 36349, Fax: 025 36781
6 Rooms, Double: €200–€270
4 Suites: €290–€340
1 Cottage: €380–€530 weekly
Dinner: €60
Open: all year, Credit cards: all major
Hidden Ireland
Country House & Self Catering

I'm impressed that Pyers O'Connor Nash's home is built on land that has belonged to his family for over 2,000 years, the ancestral home of the O'Conors of Connaught, descendants of the last High Kings of Ireland and traditional Kings of Connaught. And what a home it is, a grand 45-room Victorian Italianate mansion full of fascinating heirlooms and lovely antique furnishings. There's the coronation stone of the Kings of Connaught by the front door, Carolan's harp, rare manuscripts, and a vast array of family portraits. It could be daunting, but Pyer's and Marguerite's way of sharing their home makes it entrancing: the tremendous dining room with its Sheffield silver from the Great Exhibition, the wondrous array of books in the library, the elegant drawing room. I loved room 13, huge with its historic four-poster bed, fabulous views, and large bathroom with bath and shower; but opted for the green room, my favorite, with its tall four-poster bed and large bathroom. The former billiard room displays interesting manuscripts, and there's a small museum of lace and costumes. When the house is open to the public (June to August) guests are welcome to tag along on the 4 pm tour. On the grounds are three cottages let on a weekly, self-catering basis. Galway and Sligo are an hours drive away. *Directions:* Clonalis House is situated on the west side of Castlerea on N60.

CLONALIS HOUSE
Owners: Marguerite & Pyers O'Connor Nash
Castlerea, Co. Roscommon, Ireland
Tel & Fax: 094 9620014
4 Rooms, Double: €190–€220
3 Cottages: €350–€550 weekly
Dinner: €45 (not Sun or Mon)
Open: mid-Apr to Sept, Credit cards: MC, VS
Hidden Ireland
Country House & Self Catering

Byrne's Mal Dua House is a purpose-built guesthouse just outside Clifden. The sunny lobby doubles as a sitting room with sofas and chairs in deep-pink velour, which match the carpet and the balloon shades. An additional larger sitting room is decorated in shades of pink like the adjacent spacious dining room. All bedrooms are particularly spacious and come with different combinations of double and single beds. All have a bath or shower, hairdryer, TV, phone, trouser press, excellent reading lights, and tea- and coffee-makings. The decor is very attractive, with pastel-painted walls and coordinating drapes and bedspreads. Breakfast is the only meal served and Aideen and Peter are happy to recommend where to eat in town and arrange for a taxi to take you there. Having spent many years in the United States they are very in tune with American tastes. There's an absolute wealth of things to do in the area and Aideen and Peter will gladly help you plan your days activcities. During the third week in August, Clifden hosts the Connemara Pony Show and rooms are at a premium. *Directions:* Take the N59 from Galway to the outskirts of Clifden. Mal Dua is on your right as you enter the town.

BYRNE MAL DUA HOUSE
Owners: Aideen & Peter Byrne
Galway Road
Clifden
Connemara, Co. Galway, Ireland
Tel: 095 21171, Fax: 095 21739
14 Rooms, Double: €90–€150
Dinner: €45
Open: all year, Credit cards: all major
Guesthouse

On a sunny day there is nowhere more magical than Dolphin Beach House, set on its own 35-acre headland at the head of Clifden Bay. The views across the water to Slyne Head and Ballconneely Bay are the best that wild, untamed places can supply. Billy and Barbara tell me that their headland offers views of dolphins, seals, otters, foxes, and all kinds of seabirds. The view changes by the minute with the vagaries of the Irish weather and you can sit for hours just watching the seascape unfold. Warm weather finds guests soaking up the sun on the most private of beaches. The house was built to give views not only from the dining room and sitting room but also from several of the bedrooms—be sure to request one of these. I particularly enjoyed Bay View, and The Cove Room both tall-ceilinged room with wooden floors, king-sized beds, and French windows framing sea views. The Garden Room (no sea view) also enjoys high ceilings and its king bed faces a private garden courtyard. There is no shortage of places to eat in town—dinner is sometimes available with advanced notice. It's very much a family operation and you may well find several of the Foyles' working here. *Directions:* Take the N59 from Galway to Clifden and follow the one-way system to the top of town where you take the upper fork at the Y-junction (in front of the Alcock and Brown hotel) onto the Sky Road. After 3 km take the first left for 1 km to Dolphin Beach House.

DOLPHIN BEACH HOUSE
Owners: Barbara & Billy Foyle
Lower Sky Road
Clifden
Connemara, Co. Galway, Ireland
Tel: 095 21204, Fax: 095 22935
Toll Free: (888) 497 4138 USA
8 Rooms, Double: €165–€195
Dinner: €43
Closed: Nov 1 to mid Feb, Credit cards: MC, VS
B&B

The harbormaster certainly picked a pretty site for his home on the quay, with its wide vista of the inlet of Ardbear Bay and the town of Clifden winding up the hillside. Since 1820, Quay House has served variously as the harbormaster's home, a convent, a monastery, and a hotel. Julia and Paddy have given them a new lease of life as a stylish hotel. They decorated the whole in a refreshingly eclectic style; blending old, modern, and unconventional in an idiosyncratic way with little jokes and quirks such as Vegetarian Alley, a corridor of hunting trophies. Breakfast in the conservatory is the only meal served. For dinner, a five-minute walk brings you into town where there are several good restaurants. There are seven spacious studios, of which six have small fitted kitchens and balconies, and seven bedrooms. All rooms have spacious bathrooms with separate showers and tubs. Several are "traditional country house" in their decor, others light, fresh, and more bohemian. Particular favorites are Napoleon, a tribute room to the famous Corsican which enjoys a sitting area with panoramic views of the harbor, Out of Africa, a safari-themed studio; and The Bird Room, a studio with a few wacky stuffed parrots and a couple of large pictures featuring parrots. *Directions:* Take the N59 from Galway to Clifden and follow the one-way system to the top of the town where you take the lower fork at the first Y-junction down onto the quay.

THE QUAY HOUSE
Owners: Julia & Paddy Foyle
Beach Road
Clifden
Connemara, Co. Galway, Ireland
Tel: 095 21369, Fax: 095 21608
14 Rooms, Double: €150–€190
Open: mid-Mar to Nov, Credit cards: MC, VS
Hidden Ireland
Country House

How fortuitous that the storm of Christmas 1998 ripped off SeaMist's roof and caused such damage that only one room was habitable! This catapulted Sheila and her twin sister, whom she was visiting in California, into deciding to completely renovate this lovely old home with Sheila running it as a bed and breakfast. With her easy, friendly manner (not to mention talent at baking and jam-making), Sheila has proved a natural for the job. Add to this SeaMist's central location in Clifden and we have a real winner. Bedrooms are on the whole very spacious and accompanied by either a large bathroom or smaller shower room. Red-deal plank floors complement the warm pastel decor. For a sort of sea view, request a room at the top of the house and you'll catch a glimpse by standing on your tiptoes. Sheila's granddad was an auctioneer and some of his purchases have stayed at the house. I particularly admired the grand sideboard in the sitting room and the beautiful tall pine dresser purchased from Ballynahinch Castle. Walk out the front door and you are steps away from the main street of town with its shops, restaurants, and pubs. Drive a few yards in the other direction and you are in the lovely Connemara countryside. *Directions:* Take the N59 from Galway to Clifden and follow the one-way system to the top of town. Take a left at the square with the Alcock and Brown Hotel to the right. SeaMist is immediately on your right.

SEAMIST
Owner: Sheila Griffin
Clifden
Connemara, Co. Galway, Ireland
Tel: 095 21441
6 Rooms, Double: €80–€120
Closed: midweek in winter, Credit cards: MC, VS
B&B

Standing at the foot of the Knockmealdown mountains the Old Convent is a impressive building. Home to the Sisters of Mercy for over a hundred years Dermot and Christine Gannon have given it a complete new lease on life. Christine offers great hospitality and Dermot cooks. While the complete style of the place merits a stay THE reason to come is because of Dermot's spectacular cooking. Thursday through Sunday he presents a stunning eight course tasting menu with proper sized portions, all exquisitely cooked and beautifully presented, a divine evening long occasion. Guests are seated in the candlelit dining room, with its beautiful stained-glass windows, at around eight. o'clock. From the appetizers to the magnificent chocolate fondue we were enthralled. The same masterly talent goes into the preparation of breakfast dishes—consolation for those who are only able to stay the rest of the week. And stay you must for there is much to do in this wonderfully quiet corner of Ireland: climb the Rock of Cashel, scale the ramparts of Cahir castle, and ramble down country lanes to enjoy magnificent views from beauty spots such as the Vee. Perhaps you'll be lucky enough to come home to the room with a soaking tub perfectly placed to capture views of the mountains. *Directions:* From Cahir take the Cork road, pass the castle and take the next left for the 14km drive to Clogheen. Go through the village, turn left at the hospital sign and the convent is on your right.

THE OLD CONVENT
Owners: Christine & Dermot Gannon
Clogheen, Co. Tipperary, Ireland
Tel: 052 65565
7 Rooms, Double: €150–€190
Dinner: €60 (not Mon, Tue, Wed)
Open: all year, Credit cards: MC, VS
Country House

If you long to visit a spot off the beaten track and enjoy wonderful hospitality and divine food, you can do no better than to stay with Lucy and Johnny Madden on the Hilton Park estate. Lucy's passion is growing vegetables for the kitchen, Johnny's family home is so grand that it is hard to believe that it is a real home and not the kind where you pay a visitor's entrance fee and their son is the talented chef. It's a beautiful house of lovely rooms where guestrooms range from vast (the gorgeous Blue room and Parents room) with grand floor-to-ceiling beds, views of the lake and superb bathrooms with tubs and showers, to more modest in size, with regular-sized bathrooms containing old soaking tubs. Guests relax in the beautiful drawing room, enjoying pre-dinner drinks, conversation, and views across the terrace of formal gardens to the lake. The same enchanting view is enjoyed in the elegant dining room where guests dine at separate tables by the gentle flicker of candlelight. Breakfast is taken "below stairs" in the former servants' hall. Have your own house party by renting the entire place! Popular sightseeing includes Belleek with its pottery, Lough Erne, Castle Coole (a restored Palladian mansion), and Florence Court (a riot of rococo plasterwork). *Directions:* From the Cavan by-pass take the turnoff for Ballyhaise. Go through Ballyhaise and Scotshouse and the entrance to Hilton Park is on your left 1 km after the golf course.

HILTON PARK
Owners: Lucy & Johnny Madden
Clones
Scothouse, Co. Monaghan, Ireland
Tel: 047 56007
5 Rooms, Double: €270–€325
1 Suite: €350
Dinner: €65
Open: Apr to Sept, Credit cards: MC, VS
Hidden Ireland
Country House

Guests stopping at Rockwood House on their way north have been known to go no farther, contenting themselves with whiling away the hours in this peaceful spot and enjoying the warm hospitality that Susan and James McCauley offer. Susan and James returned here after living in Dublin for many years, acquired a derelict rectory with trees growing through the roof, and replaced it with a well-appointed replica-Rockwood House. Enjoy breakfast in the conservatory overlooking the garden or just relax around the fire in the guests sitting room. For dinner guests have a choice of restaurants in Belturbert, to the Derragarra Inn just down the road in Butlersbridge or, for scrumptious more pricey fare, the adjacent Olde Post Restaurant. Upstairs, the spacious, very nicely decorated bedrooms are each accompanied by a snug bathroom. Beds are double, twin, or king if you request that the twin beds be zipped together. County Cavan is blessed with picture-postcard scenery—whichever way you turn you find waterways, rivers, and lakes set among gently rolling hills. Opportunities for fishing and walking abound. Popular sightseeing includes Belleek Pottery, Lough Erne, Castle Coole (a restored Palladian mansion), and Florence Court (a riot of rococo plaster). *Directions:* From Cavan follow signs for the N3 to Monaghan, then turn right at the sign for Monaghan/Butlersbridge (N54). Rockwood House is on your left, 3 km from the village of Butlersbridge.

🍺 ⚿ @ P 🚭 🍴 👭 🐎

ROCKWOOD HOUSE
Owners: Susan & James McCauley
Cloverhill
Belturbet, Co. Cavan, Ireland
Tel: 047 55351, Fax: 047 55373
4 Rooms, Double: €64
Closed: Dec 10 to Feb 1, Credit cards: none
B&B

Set high above the river surrounded by over three acres of grounds this grand 1840s Victorian commands an impressive position in Cobh—but the main point of interest is the fabulous interior as Pam and John spared no expense in revamping their longtime home into luxury guest accommodation. Their easy hospitality, as much as the comfort of their lovely home, is what makes Knockeven House special. Your stay often begins with tea and scones by the drawing room fire. Up the grand curving staircase you find the airy bedrooms—three have six foot beds (can also be twin), and one has a queen. Showers are large, bedrooms are wired for internet access, and TVs are available. Scrambled eggs and smoked salmon is a breakfast specialty. Favorite activities are: visiting the cathedral and Queenstown Story a lively museum illustrating emigration to the US from 1845 to the 1950s; taking the ferry to Kinsale; going to Blarney to kiss the famous stone; and visiting the English market and shops in nearby Cork. John, an avid golfer, is a mine of information on local courses and happy to arranges tee times. *Directions:* Just before you arrive in Cork (from N25—Waterford to Cork Road) turn left on R624 to Cobh. On entering Cobh, pass the ferry on your right. At Satoil garage take a sharp left and an immediate right into the Knockeven House's driveway.

KNOCKEVEN HOUSE
Owners: Pam & John Mulhaire
Rushbrooke
Cobh, Co. Cork, Ireland
Tel: 021 4811778, Fax: 021 4811719
4 Rooms, Double: €120–€130
Open: all year, Credit cards: MC, VS
B&B

The charm of Greenhill House is that Elizabeth and James Hegarty are particularly sweet people who have been welcoming guests to their house for many years. They are particularly knowledgeable about the area and happy to direct guests on where to go and what to see—of course the nearby Antrim coast is particularly popular. Elizabeth makes sure you are always welcomed with tea and cakes and have everything that you need. The farmhouse is delightfully old-fashioned and lovingly decorated with antiques, with bouquets of fresh garden flowers adding the finishing touch. Bedrooms are well equipped with sightseeing information; a tray set with teapot, kettle, tea bags, coffee, and chocolate; hairdryer; television; and even a little box of After Eight mints by the bedside. Plump comforters top the beds and fluffy towels hang on the old-fashioned towel rail. One the main floor you find a double and twin room with their bathrooms cleverly popped into snug "fitted" cupboards: a shower in one and a sink and toilet in another. Bedrooms under the eaves have more spacious bathrooms. A bountiful breakfast is the only meal served and Elizabeth will suggest restaurants round and about for dinner. *Directions:* From Limavady take the A37 towards Coleraine, turn right on the A29 (Garvagh and Cookstown road) for 11 km. Turn left on the B66 (Greenhill Road) and Greenhill House is on the right.

GREENHILL HOUSE
Owners: Elizabeth & James Hegarty
24 Greenhill Road
Coleraine, BT51 4EU, Northern Ireland
Tel: 028 7086 8241, Fax: 028 7086 8365
6 Rooms, Double: £60
Open: Mar to Oct, Credit cards: MC, VS
Farmhouse B&B

Mary and Declan Kelleher like nothing more than to share their love of the Burren with visitors. They have gone so far as to compile a most interesting booklet on the district, which details its history and points of interest. To make sure you do not go wrong they will kit you out with maps and instructions on what to do each day. Fergus View was built as a teacher's residence at the turn of the last century and Declan's grandfather was its first occupant. Continuing in his grandfather's footsteps, Declan is the principal of Corofin's primary school. The next generation of teachers is in place with several of Mary and Declan's children training to be teachers. In an evening the fire is lit in the little parlor to encourage you to make yourself at home. A hearty breakfast is the only meal served but handily there's a restaurant in the village for dinner. Bedrooms are prettily decorated with matching drapes and bedspreads. All are of the leave-large-cases-in-the-car variety—facilities are not designed for persons of large proportions. The Kellehers also have a lovely self-catering cottage for week-long stays. The nearby Burren is fascinating, and the Cliffs of Moher are close at hand. *Directions:* From Shannon airport take the N18 to Ennis, the N85 towards Lisdoonvarna, turn first right to Corofin, go through the village, and the house is on your left after 3 km.

FERGUS VIEW
Owners: Mary & Declan Kelleher
Corofin
Kilnaboy, Co. Clare, Ireland
Tel: 065 6837606, Fax: 065 6837192
6 Rooms, Double: €76–€78
1 Cottage: €400–€630 weekly
Open: mid-Mar to mid-Oct, Credit cards: none
B&B & Self Catering

St. Clerans has had an impressive list of Irish owners but came into the limelight when John Huston (film director extraordinaire) called it home for over 20 years and spent an absolute mint on the place. More recently this impressive home prepared itself for the 21st century with another no-holds-barred face-lift from former chat-show host Merv Griffin who designed it as his luxurious retreat. It's a treat to see an architectural gem coddled to the extent where everything is the absolute best that money can buy—the essence of pure indulgence. My personal favorite room is Merv's former suite—you can unpack into the closet he used and admire the artwork that Merv placed in the niches that once held John Houston's Oscars. The most private bedroom is the octagonal little building that was once Angelica Huston's playhouse. She would not recognize it today with its stenciled walls and opulent bathroom. Spend the day lounging on the premises soaking up the ambiance and being totally spoiled by the attentive Irish staff, play golf at Athenry and Loughrea, or go horseriding or clay pigeon shooting. The cliffs of Moher on the Burren and Galway city are within easy striking distance. *Directions:* From Galway take the N6 towards Dublin for 30 km to Craughwell. Go through the village and take the second left signposted St. Clerans and Athenry for the 8-km drive to St. Clerans.

ST. CLERANS
Manager: Barry Kilroy
Craughwell, Co Galway, Ireland
Tel: 091 846555, Fax: 091 846752
12 Rooms, Double: €225–€475
Dinner: €70
Open: all year, Credit cards: all major
Country House Hotel

Enniscoe House is the home of Susan Kellett—a descendant of the original family who settled this estate in the 1670s—her son DJ, and their Labrador Frodo. Staying as her guest gives you a glimpse of what it was like to live in a grand country mansion—the old family furniture, portraits, books, and family memorabilia are yours to enjoy. The lofty rooms are decorated true to the Georgian period and all are in tiptop condition. The three front bedrooms, of grand proportions, are reached by a grand elliptical staircase. Those in the older part of the house are less grand but just as lovely. I particularly enjoyed the old nursery with half-tester and twin beds, and comfortable chintz chairs. Dinners by soft, flickering candlelight at little tables in the large dining room are a real treat. Tucked behind the house, the courtyard buildings house three delightful farmhouse-style self-catering apartments. The Victorian walled garden has been given a new lease of life and the barns display old farm machinery and artifacts. Fishery manager Gary Crossley offers help to anglers fishing Lough Conn (email: gary@cloonamoynefishery.com). Walk the trails that go through the woodlands past the forestry plantations and along the lake shore. There are great cliffs along the north coast, where the Stone-Age settlements at Céide Fields have been excavated. *Directions:* From Ballina take the N59 to Crossmolina, turn left in town for Castlebar, and the house is on the left after 3 km.

ENNISCOE HOUSE
Owners: Susan & DJ Kellett
Castlehill
Crossmolina, Co. Mayo, Ireland
Tel: 096 31112, Fax: 096 31773
6 Rooms, Double: €192–€240
3 Cottages: €600–€900 weekly
Dinner: €50
Open: Apr to mid-Oct, Credit cards: MC, VS
Ireland's Blue Book
Country House & Self Catering

Mary and John Curran are locals who built Greenmount House as a home for themselves and their small children then later cleverly expanded their bungalow adding a large sitting room, additional family accommodation, and large top-of-the-line guestrooms. Seven face the harbor and six have either French windows opening onto a patio or balcony (chairs provided for sitting out) and are large enough to accommodate a spacious sitting area—the kind of rooms you want to spend time in. Drift into the view in room 6 (Garran) whose bed and sofa face a breathtaking vista of Connor Pass soaring above the fields. A conservatory breakfast room, prettily furnished with painted pine furniture, has a panoramic view across fields and Dingle's rooftops to the harbor. Mary prepares the most bountiful of breakfasts and tries to offer at least two fruit dishes, delicious mueslis, and yogurts, as well as a cooked breakfast menu that includes not only the traditional breakfast but also fish and mushrooms in yogurt sauce. Breakfast is the only meal served. For dinner stroll down the hill into town where there are some particularly fine fish restaurants. Wander down to the harbor and watch the catch come in, window shop, and enjoy a pint in one of the many pubs. *Directions:* Turn right at the roundabout in Dingle, next right into John Street, and continue up the hill to Greenmount House.

■ ⚡🛏️ CREDIT 🕿 @ W ⍣ P ⚓ 🛶 🚶 🐎 🏄

GREENMOUNT HOUSE
Owners: Mary & John Curran
Gortonora
Dingle, Co Kerry, Ireland
Tel: 066 9151414, Fax: 066 9151974
14 Rooms, Double: €100–€170
Closed: Christmas, Credit cards: MC, VS
B&B

Heaton's, a purpose-built guesthouse, commands an enviable position at the head of Dingle Bay, with spectacular views across the water to Burnham Headlands. The mouth of the sheltered harbor is just a five-minute walk from the heart of this lively town. While the style outside is modern, the inside is more traditional with classic French furniture. The bedrooms are smartly decorated with beds coming in sizes from twin to king. Nuala is a stickler for quality when it comes to bedding and towels, so crisp white sheets adorn the beds and good-quality towels hang in the sparkling white bathrooms, which all have power showers over the tubs. Ten of the rooms have views to the bay and three are large enough to accommodate a second bed for a child (request a second-floor room for the best view). Rooms 14 and 16 are the most spacious of rooms, with a king-sized bed, roomy sitting area, and Jacuzzi tub and shower. Daughter Jackie, the breakfast chef, makes certain breakfast is a full Irish spread of local produce, with the fish and omelettes, made with free-range eggs, deserving a special mention. *Directions:* Arriving in Dingle, keep the harbor to your left and Heaton's is located 600 yards beyond the marina on your right, overlooking the bay.

HEATON'S
Owners: Nuala, Jackie & Cameron Heaton
The Wood
Dingle, Co Kerry, Ireland
Tel: 066 9152288, Fax: 066 9152324
14 Rooms, Double: €94–€138
2 Suites: €130–€190
Open: all year, Credit cards: MC, VS
Guesthouse

Set on a wooded, tidal island in Donegal Bay and joined to the mainland by a narrow causeway, St. Ernan's House was built in 1826 by John Hamilton, a nephew of the Duke of Wellington, for his wife. Over lunch here one day, Brian and Carmel O'Dowd decided that St. Ernan's was the kind of hotel they would like to own, so several years later when it came on the market they took the plunge and forsook their careers in banking and teaching to become hoteliers. From almost every one of the rooms you are treated to marvelous views across a mirrorlike span of water. In the lounge, window seats offer views across the water to the mainland and chairs are artfully arranged to provide numerous nooks for intimate after-dinner conversation. A four-course candlelit dinner, with choices for each course, is served in the dining room. The attractive bedrooms come in all shapes and sizes, and while almost all have delightful water views, the largest command the highest prices. Be sure to enjoy the walk around this delightful little island. You'll find some excellent shops in Donegal town, amongst them Magees, famous for its tweed. Beyond Donegal town lies the wild, rugged landscape that has made this county famous. *Directions:* From Sligo take the N15 towards Donegal as far as the village of Laghey (6.5 km before Donegal). Approximately 1.5 km past Laghey take the left-hand turn onto R267. Proceed for 1.6 km and St. Ernan's is signposted to your left.

ST. ERNAN'S HOUSE
Owners: Carmel & Brian O'Dowd
Donegal, Co Donegal, Ireland
Tel: 074 9721065, Fax: 074 9722098
6 Rooms, Double: €230–€290
3 Suites: €330
Dinner: €52 (Fri & Sat only)
Open: mid-Apr to Oct, Credit cards: MC, VS
Ireland's Blue Book
Country House Hotel

"What a great place to have a party!" I exclaimed—and the thought had not escaped former owners, for there are tales in the town of grand parties long ago with guests dancing in the expansive drawing and dining rooms and a quartet in the back hallway. These aristocratic rooms have been restored to their former glory, with a wedding-cake icing of plasterwork ringing their lofty ceilings above sink-in sofas and chairs and a vast dining-room table. Upstairs has received the same sensitive treatment. The two premier rooms at the front of the house have vast bathrooms with large tubs and separate showers and enough room in the bedrooms to accommodate seating by the fire and a couple of beds. Between them stands an extra bedroom (without bath), ideal for an older child or traveling companion. The fourth bedroom overlooks the courtyard. For dinner guests usually drive to local restaurants. With advance notice Laura will prepare supper. Michael and Laura find that many guests are interested in their restoration and often give a tour of "behind the scenes" portions of the property. *Directions:* From Mallow take the N20 towards Limerick for 6.5 km to New Twopothouse. Turn right for the 6.5-km drive to Doneraile where you find Creagh House on your left at the far end of the main street.

CREAGH HOUSE
Owners: Laura O'Mahony & Michael O'Sullivan
Main Street
Doneraile, Co Cork, Ireland
Tel: 022 24433, Fax: 022 24715
4 Rooms, Double: €200–€240
Supper: €30
Open: Mar to Oct, Credit cards: all major
Hidden Ireland
Country House

The heart of Temple Bar with its trendy stores and vibrant nightlife is a most appropriate spot for a luxury boutique hotel. Originally built in 1852, the building was for many years a cleric's residence. The conversion to a hotel kept all the attractive architectural features such as oak paneling, wooden floors, and lovely old windows. The cleric colors of purple, brown, red, blue, and gold are subtly included in every room. Decor is uncluttered, with simple lines. Relax in the peace and quiet of the study with its open fire, writing table, and wood-paneled walls or enjoy conviviality and a cocktail in the Octagon Bar. The Tea Room, a onetime ballroom with magnificent art deco windows, is a grand place to eat dinner. Bedrooms and bathrooms have lots of lovely, mellow American White Oak, Egyptian cotton bedding and splashes of blue, brown, red or gold—all very serene—and double glazing ensures a quiet night's sleep. The handcrafted beds are king sized and rooms are equipped with interactive TV, entertainment systems, and wifi. There are seven balcony rooms, and several rooms that interconnect to make two bedroom family suites—children are made particularly welcome. The location, overlooking the River Liffey on Dublin's "left bank" is perfect for exploring Dublin on foot. The hotel has a small garage and valet parking is available. *Directions:* Wellington Quay is on the south bank of the River Liffey—see Dublin Walking Tour map.

THE CLARENCE
Manager: Olivier Sevestre
6–8 Wellington Quay
Dublin, Co. Dublin, Ireland
Tel: 01 4070800, Fax: 01 4070820
49 Rooms, Double: €350–€2800
Closed: Christmas, Credit cards: all major
City Hotel

Grand as life in Georgian Dublin may have been, it is surpassed at The Merrion, a dream of a hotel found in the heart of the city opposite Leinster House, home of Ireland's parliament. A few steps from bustling city streets and you are in vast drawing rooms enjoying traditional afternoon tea overlooking a tranquil expanse of garden and watching the gardener manicure the box hedges. If you are in the mood for the most sophisticated of meals, adjourn to the two-Michelin-star restaurant Patrick Guilbaud or enjoy more traditional Irish cuisine in The Cellar Restaurant after letting your hair down over a few drinks in The Cellar Bar which lists over 50 wines by the glass on its menu. The Tethra Spa is an aptly named spot to assist guests in recovering from the revelry of the night before—swimming in the pool, working out in the gym, or enjoying a massage. It costs a good deal to stay in one of the elegant suites in the "old building" while more affordable accommodation is found in the deluxe garden wing whose most attractive rooms open up to views of the loveliest of gardens. The hotel has the largest collection of Irish art outside the National Gallery. A traditional hotel in the heart of this vibrant city—what more could you ask from a place to stay? *Directions:* The Merrion is adjacent to Merrion Square, opposite Leinster House. Park in front of the hotel and the porter will take care of your car. See Dublin Walking Tour map for location.

✻ ⚗ 💳 ☎ ⚰ 🏹 @ 𝐘 P 🍴 🚭 ☘ 🌊 🖼 ⚘ ⚒ ⚓ 🤺 🏇 ⚓

THE MERRION
Manager: Peter MacCann
Upper Merrion Street
Dublin, Co. Dublin, Ireland
Tel: 01 6030600, Fax: 01 6030700
138 Rooms, Double: €495–€950*
5 Suites: €825–€3000*
*Breakfast not included: €24–€29
Dinner: €55
Open: all year, Credit cards: all major
City Hotel

Modern hotels are not usually included in this guide, but I was so taken with the value for money and excellent location offered by the Mespil Hotel that I decided to stay there, and I was very pleased with the quality of the accommodation and the friendliness of the staff. Sitting beside the Grand Canal with its grassy verges and leafy trees, the Mespil sports a pleasing modern exterior that complements its attractive contemporary interior. Stylish sofas and chairs deck the lobby while the adjacent restaurant, all decked out in light wood, offers a bistro-style menu The bar with its clubby chairs and sofas offers a very popular carvery lunch. Bedrooms come in three varieties—front, back and side. Front rooms face the canal (opt for one of these as it's a treat to have a view room in Dublin), while back and side rooms offer complete peace and quiet. Nearly all of the bedrooms offer one queen and one single bed. From the hotel it is a 15 minute walk to St Stephens Green. *Directions:* Follow signs for South City to Baggot Street. Cross the canal, turn right, and the Mespil is on your left after 200 meters. The hotel has 50 parking spaces available on a first come first served basis. See Dublin Walking Tour map for location.

MESPIL HOTEL
Manager: Martin Holohan
Mespil Road
Ballsbridge
Dublin, Co. Dublin, Ireland
Tel: 01 4884600, Fax: 01 6671244
255 Rooms, Double: €105–€215*
*Breakfast not included: €13
Dinner: from €30
Closed: Dec 24 to 26, Credit cards: all major
City Hotel

A tall, creeper-covered wall and a discreet plaque are the only indications that you have arrived at 31 Leeson Close an absolutely top of the line bed and breakfast. Ring the buzzer, open the tall doors, and you enter an oasis of tranquility and greenery far from the clamor of the surrounding city. Number 31 was home to Ireland's famous 60s modern architect, Sam Stephenson, who fashioned it from two coach houses. Noel and Deirdre Comer, the present owners, have kept the cool, clean lines of this modern home. A contemporary painting hangs above the fireplace in the living room where the leather sofa, the only piece of furniture, hugs the wall of the conversation pit and stark, whitewashed brick walls contrast texturally with the mosaic tiled floor. Beautiful bedrooms and their accompanying luxury bathrooms are spread over two buildings—the décor is minimalist the quality of beds, bedding and toiletries luxurious. The main house has grand, high-ceilinged rooms, while the coach house naturally has lower-ceilinged rooms, several of which have their own private patio. Noel, Deirdre, and Homer (the Labrador) work hard to give a gracious welcome and (Homer excluded) provide you with all the information you need on what to see and where to go in Dublin. *Directions:* Lower Leeson Street runs off the southern end of St. Stephen's Green. Leeson Close is opposite 41 Lower Leeson Street. A secure, off-road car park is adjacent to Number 31.

NUMBER 31
Owners: Deirdre & Noel Comer
31 Leeson Close
Dublin, Co. Dublin, Ireland
Tel: 01 6765011, Fax: 01 6762929
21 Rooms, Double: €140–€330
Open: all year, Credit cards: all major
Hidden Ireland
Guesthouse

When it first opened in the heart of Dublin in 1824, The Shelbourne offered a suitably handsome "home away from home" for Irish nobility and landed gentry. Today, this legendary grande dame welcomes a wider spectrum of guests–including the city's politicians and literati–but is still the place to stay, a luxurious, elegant hotel that easily lives up to its maxim as "the most distinguished address in Ireland." The comings and goings of Dublin socialites are reflected in the enormous mirror in the lobby as they pass on their way to the Lord Mayor's Lounge for afternoon tea, to the lively Horseshoe Bar for cocktails, to the contemporary Saddle Room for steak and seafood, or for a drink overlooking St. Stephen's Green in Number 27 Bar and Lounge. The beautifully appointed bedrooms include 19 suites, each named after a famous guest. You might consider treating yourself to the Princess Grace Suite, an opulent two-bedroom affair favored by the princess on her visits to Dublin. And be sure to visit the Constitution Room (known then as Room 112), which played an important role in the founding of the Irish nation), as it was here that the Irish Constitution was drafted in 1922. *Directions:* The Shelbourne is on the north side of St. Stephen's Green. Park in front to unload and your car will be taken to the hotel's garage. See Dublin Walking Tour map for location.

THE SHELBOURNE
Manager: Liam Doyle
27 St. Stephen's Green
Dublin, Co. Dublin, Ireland
Tel: 01 6634500, Fax: 01 6616006
265 Rooms, Double: €215–€2700*
*Breakfast not included: €29
Open: all year, Credit cards: all major
City Hotel

Waterloo House is two tall Georgian townhomes cleverly combined to become a delightful guesthouse. Just a 15-minute walk to St. Stephen's Green and Trinity College, it is well set back from one of Dublin's quieter streets and has parking in front. Evelyn Corcoran and her friendly staff really try hard to look after their guests. Soft strains of classical music play in the lobby sitting room and there's an elevator for luggage and for those who do not want to climb as many as four flights of stairs. Whether your bedroom is on the garden level or at the top of the house, you'll be pleased with its smart décor. Rooms are cozy in size with king bedded rooms, overlooking the garden, being the most spacious. Breakfast is taken downstairs in the breakfast room that opens up to a sunny conservatory and gardens. Keycards give you access to the front door as well as your room so that you can come and go on your own timetable. There are lots of restaurants and bars within easy walking distance and Evelyn has comprised a "guide" giving useful eatery recommendations and pricing. *Directions:* Follow signs for South City. Cross the Baggot Street Bridge into Baggot Street. Pass a row of shops on your left and turn right into Waterloo Road—Waterloo House is on your left with a car park in front. See Dublin Walking Tour map for location.

WATERLOO HOUSE
Owner: Evelyn Corcoran
8–10 Waterloo Road
Ballsbridge
Dublin, Co. Dublin, Ireland
Tel: 01 6601888, Fax: 01 6671955
19 Rooms, Double: €115–€250
Open: all year, Credit cards: MC, VS
Guesthouse

Dating back to 1698, Grange Lodge is one of those large, comfortable houses that have evolved as owners have added and altered over the years. Today it's the home of Norah and Ralph Brown, easygoing, friendly folk who offer guests the warmest of welcomes. Norah has won many awards for her outstandingly good food and runs regular cooking classes. Be sure to book dinner when you make your reservations. Norah serves coffee in the lovely drawing room or in the den, a cozy room where, on colder evenings, a log fire bids a cheery welcome. The Browns are inveterate collectors and as a consequence lovely furniture, old china, pewter, stoneware, and fascinating bygones fill every nook and cranny. Upstairs are the very comfortable, individually decorated bedrooms, all with their own pretty bathrooms full of little extras. Acres of gardens ensure peace and quiet though it's just a minute's drive to main roads, making this an ideal touring base for the northern counties. Tour the nearby Tyrone crystal factory and try your own hand at cutting the hand-blown sparkling crystal. Nearby are two National Trust properties: Ardress House, a 17th-century manor, and The Argory, an 1820s house with a lot of original furniture. *Directions:* Take the M1 from Belfast to junction 15, take the A29 towards Armagh for 2 km, turn left at the Grange Lodge sign. Turn almost immediately right and Grange Lodge is the first white-walled entrance on the right.

GRANGE LODGE
Owners: Norah & Ralph Brown
7 Grange Road
Dungannon, BT71 7EJ, Northern Ireland
Tel: 028 8778 4212, Fax: 028 8778 4313
5 Rooms, Double: £85–£89
Dinner: from £32 (not Sun)
Open: Feb to mid-Dec, Credit cards: MC, VS
Country House

Ann and Jim Mulligan built An Bohreen high on a hill with fabulous views. From the outside, it looks like a conventional bungalow; but once you are inside the dining room, you are presented with a wall of windows overlooking the bay of Dungarvan. The sitting room windows frame the Comeragh Mountains. Bedrooms are fresh and pretty with antique dressers and attractive bed linen. Jim is quintessentially Irish with a gleam in his eye, and a natural friendliness. He carries your bag, plans sightseeing, and answers questions; while Ann has a reputation for excellent cooking. A dinner here may well be the highlight of your trip. The four-course dinner must be reserved 24 hours in advance and is often wild salmon or Waterford lamb. Breakfasts are a real treat with warm scones and fresh-squeezed juice preceding the cooked dish with choices such as crepes with sautéed apples or the traditional "full Irish." Main roads will whisk you off to Waterford for sightseeing. You can stay close to home, visit local potteries, go hill walking or riding. Of course, you must see the local fairy bush covered with ribbons and bits that folks decorate it with. You drive your car down the hill, stop at the fairy bush, and your car starts to reverse up the hill on its own. Jim assures me it happens every time. *Directions:* From Waterford take the N25 towards Cork. Make a right turn 5 km from the "Resume Speed" sign as you leave the hamlet of Lemybrien.

AN BOHREEN
Owners: Ann & Jim Mulligan
Killeneen West
Dungarvan, Co. Waterford, Ireland
Tel: 051 291010, Fax: 051 291011
4 Rooms, Double: €90–€95
Dinner: €38 (not Tue, Wed, Thu)
Open: mid-Mar to Nov, Credit cards: MC, VS
B&B

You'll enjoy staying at Powersfield House on the outskirts of Dungarvan. Eunice has decorated her home with great style, she's a talented chef, and a warm, easy going person. When Eunice returned to Dungarvan to marry a local farmer they built this substantial neo-Georgian home large enough to provide plenty of space for their family on one side of the house and guests on the other. There are six most attractive bedrooms decorated with a modern flair in a traditional country house style. Downstairs guests have a comfortable sitting room adjacent to the dining room. Eunice is a talented chef who, until she had 3 young boys, ran a popular restaurant. Now she limits herself to dinner for guests though she is happy to give day-long cookery courses to parties of guests, demonstrating an arsenal of easy to prepare dishes for entertaining. Just down the road Dungarven is an attractive seaside town round a pretty bay. It's a particularly attractive coastal drive to Waterford and you can return by a faster, inland route. To the west is Ardmore, a 7th century monastic settlement. *Directions:* From Dungarvan take the Clonmel road. Powersfield House is the second turn to the left, and the first house on the right.

POWERSFIELD HOUSE
Owners: Eunice & Edmund Power
Ballinamuck
Dungarvan, Co. Waterford, Ireland
Tel: 058 45594, Fax: 058 45550
6 Rooms, Double: €110–€125
Dinner: €27–€37
Open: all year, Credit cards: all major
Country House

The summertime evening view from the dining room of Castle Murray House is simply staggering. As the night slowly draws in on green fields that tumble to the sea and scudding clouds dapple the reddening sky, the sun slowly sinks behind the distant Slieve League, the highest sea cliffs in Europe. The food, with lots of local seafood on the menu, is as outstanding as the view and served in portions that satisfy even the heartiest of Irish appetites. Chef Remy Dupuy's cooking attracts a large local following, so the best way to secure an often hard-to-come-by dinner reservation is to stay here. After an evening-long repast you can retire up the narrow pine staircase to one of the smartly decorated bedrooms with their sprightly contemporary decor and pleasing color schemes. Be sure to request a room with a view of the bay. If you want the most spacious of accommodation, opt for the "honeymoon room" found atop a narrow flight of stairs at the top of the house. While it does not have "the view" from its bedroom, it does from its spacious deck. Between breakfast and dinner the rugged Donegal landscape is yours to explore. *Directions:* From Donegal take the N56 towards Killybegs. The left-hand turn to Castle Murray House is after Dunkineely.

CASTLE MURRAY HOUSE HOTEL & RESTAURANT
Owner: Marguerite Howley
Manager: Jorg Demmerer
Dunkineely, Co. Donegal, Ireland
Tel: 074 9737022, Fax: 074 9737330
10 Rooms, Double: €130–€150
Dinner: €50–€65
Closed: Christmas & mid-Jan to mid-Feb
Credit cards: MC, VS
Restaurant With Rooms

Joe and Kay O'Flynn bought Rathsallagh House, a converted Queen Anne stables with 530 acres of farmland, in 1978. Encouraged by the spaciousness of the house, Kay opened three rooms for bed and breakfast guests and thus began a venture that has evolved into the country house hotel and golf club that you see today. Tractor sheds and barns are gone, replaced by a parade of bedrooms, and fields that lined the driveway are now the groomed fairways of a championship golf course rated one of the top 30 in Ireland. The billiard room, tennis court, Jacuzzi, sauna and capacious gardens encourage total relaxation. While the size of the operation makes it all seem rather grand, Rathsallagh manages to keep the bonhomie of a friendly, relaxed country house hotel complete with homey touches like turf and log fires in the drawing rooms. Begin the day with a lavish breakfast, choosing from an array of savory dishes on the sideboard. Relax with a drink and then enjoy your dinner which features fresh local produce, herbs and vegetables from Rathsallagh's gardens. Realize that you deserve the best and stay in one of the deluxe stable rooms. It's just a 45 minute drive to the K Club where the Ryder Cup was held in 2006. Sightseeing includes the Wicklow Mountains, Glendalough, and the National Stud. *Directions:* From Dublin airport take the M50 south then the N7, which you exit for the M9 (Carlow). After 9.5 km pass the Priory Inn on the left and just over 3 km later turn left for Rathsallagh.

RATHSALLAGH HOUSE
Owner: The O'Flynn family
Dunlavin, Co Wicklow, Ireland
Tel: 045 403112, Fax: 045 403343
29 Rooms, Double: €280–€330
Dinner: €65
Open: all year, Credit cards: all major
Country House Hotel

Farran House is a large, elegant 18th century, Italianate style, manor house situated in the Lee valley, overlooking the medieval castle and abbey of Kilcrea. John and Patricia have completed a painstaking restoration and they now live in a wing while guests rent the main house on a self-catering basis. Relax round the fire in the sitting room, enjoy a game of billiards in the former music room, and chat with family and friends round the dining-room table. Upstairs, you find four lovely, spacious bedrooms all enjoying south-facing views across the valley. One room is extra special because of its bathroom—a super-sized affair with a claw-foot tub sitting center stage. Your hosts have collected a picture library of all things Ireland—they travel the length and breadth of the country taking photos, which gives them an intimate knowledge of every scenic spot in the country—very handy for advising where to go and what to see. Blarney is 16 kilometers away, Kinsale and the coast about 40 kilometers. *Directions:* From Cork take the N22 towards Killarney for 15 km. Go around Ballincollig on the ring road and, after Dan Sheanhan's pub on your right, take the second right. Take the next right up the hill and the first gate is on your left.

FARRAN HOUSE
Owners: Patricia Wiese & John Kehely
Farran, Co. Cork, Ireland
Tel: 021 7331215
1 House: €3500–€4800 weekly
Open: Apr to Oct, Credit cards: all major
Hidden Ireland
Self Catering

Desmond, the 29th Knight of Glin's demesne is a 400-acre farm and late-18th-century castle stretching along the banks of the River Shannon. Staying here affords you the opportunity to live luxuriously—the house is an absolute beauty, full of exquisite furniture, family portraits, and beautiful artifacts. It is all very grand but not at all stuffy, for your host is Bob Duff, a gregarious New Zealander who ensures that you are well taken care of and well fed. He will give you a tour of the house with lots of suitably embellished stories. If you are passionate about art, literature, furniture, or books, be sure to ask if the Knight is in residence, for Desmond is happy to meet with guests when he is at home. Sip tea in the grand drawing room or curl up with a good book in the oh-so-comfortable sitting room. Bedrooms range from large and luxurious with extra-large bathrooms and dressing rooms to small and, by comparison, more ordinary. Ballybunion golf course is close at hand and the new Greg Norman-designed links course Doonbeg is an hour away via the Tarbert car ferry. *Directions:* From Limerick take the N69 towards Tralee for 50 km to Glin. At the end of the village turn left following the estate's wall to the castle entrance.

GLIN CASTLE
Owners: Olda & Desmond FitzGerald, Knight of Glin
Manager: Bob Duff
Glin, Co Limerick, Ireland
Tel: 068 34173, Fax: 068 34364
15 Rooms, Double: €320–€510
Dinner: €60
Closed: Nov to Mar, Credit cards: all major
Ireland's Blue Book
Country House Hotel

This dazzling, three-story Regency house, formerly the dower house of the Courtown estate, has an atmosphere of refined elegance created by vivacious hostess Mary Bowe and her delightful daughters Margaret and Laura. Mary has great charm and energy—during our stay she chatted with guests before dinner, made the rounds during dinner, and was back again at breakfast checking up to make certain that everything was perfect. The house is full of antiques, classic pieces that transport you back to the days of gracious living in grand houses. While we especially enjoyed our large, twin-bedded room with impressive, well-polished furniture, elegant decor, and a grand bathroom, I found the other bedrooms equally attractive. Six prized units are the ultra-luxurious, gorgeously decorated, extravagantly priced State Rooms tucked away in a separate ground-floor wing: request the Print Suite, Stopford, Georgian, or French. Dinner is served in the ornate conservatory dining room—all greenery and mirrors. The food is a delight—superb French and Irish dishes. *Directions:* Marlfield House is 88 km from Dublin. Take the N11 south to Gorey and exit at exit 23. Follow signs for Courtown and turn left at Courtown Road roundabout. Marlfield is on the left hand side after 1km..

MARLFIELD HOUSE
Owners: Mary, Margaret, Laura & Bowe
Courtown Road
Gorey, Co Wexford, Ireland
Tel: 053 9421124, Fax: 053 9421572
13 Rooms, Double: €210–€275
6 Suites: €405–€765
Dinner: €65–€75
Closed: late Dec to Feb 1, Credit cards: all major
Relais & Châteaux
Country House Hotel

As newlyweds, Philomena and her husband John put in an exceedingly low bid on a very tumbledown Woodlands Farmhouse and it was many years before she found out why their offer had been accepted. To hear why and enjoy intriguing tales of gold sovereigns, cursed families, and arranged marriages, you will have to go and stay and ask Philomena for a story session with tea or coffee and scones upon arrival. What started out as a simple bed and breakfast has now grown into a very professional guesthouse. Guests have a cozily cluttered parlor with an eclectic assortment of sizeable Victorian chairs. The parlor opens up to an expansive dining room lit by two grand crystal chandeliers, which overlooks the lovely back garden. The front garden is even more impressive: a grand sweep of lawn with shrubs and trees going down to the river and the tennis court. All the smartly decorated bedrooms enjoy garden views and range in size from large family rooms to snug twins—all have electric blankets and small en suite shower or bathrooms with hairdryers. Room 6 is a particularly spacious room overlooking the back garden. In Wexford you can visit Wexford Heritage Park or Johnstown Castle Museum. To the north lies the Vale of Avoca. *Directions:* Take exit 22 for Gorey (Turnock roundabout) you will see the sign immediately for Woodlands Country House on the right. Located 1 mile off the N11 and 4 miles from the town of Gorey—a 6 minutes drive.

WOODLANDS COUNTRY HOUSE
Owner: Philomena O'Sullivan
Gorey
Killinierin, Co. Wexford, Ireland
Tel: 0402 37125, Fax: 0402 37133
6 Rooms, Double: €110–€130
Open: Apr to Oct, Credit cards: MC, VS
Guesthouse

This is not your "Hollywood" of frantic freeways and homes of the rich and famous—this is the County Down version: a very nice town facing the sea backed by pastoral countryside. Here Beech Hill House, a Georgian-style dower house built for Victoria's grandmother, sits atop a little knoll. As we sat in the conservatory enjoying tea and fruitcake, I found it hard to believe that half an hour earlier I had been in the heart of Belfast. Victoria grew up just down the road on what is now the site of the Ulster Folk Museum so she is an expert on what to see and do in the area. She also has a real flair for decorating and her lovely home is filled with enviable family furniture. Bedrooms are on the ground floor and have all the right stuff: lovely furniture, books, hairdryers, TVs, goodies, firm beds (a zip-link twin/king, a double, and a queen), fine Irish linen, and well-proportioned bathrooms. We were up at dawn for a flight and Victoria insisted that we start our day with a "little" breakfast: the sideboard was groaning with bowls of fruit, yogurt, and fresh-baked bread accompanied by homemade jam...and then we moved on to the cooked items! For week long stays consider the Colonel's Lodge, a two-bedroom cottage in the garden. *Directions:* Leave Belfast on the A2 in the direction of Bangor. Bypass Holywood and about 2.5 km after going under the bridge at the Ulster Folk Museum turn right signed to Craigantlet. Beech Hill House is 3 km along on the left.

BEECH HILL COUNTRY HOUSE
Owner: Victoria Brann
23 Ballymoney Road
Craigantlet
Holywood, BT23 4TG, Northern Ireland
Tel: 028 9042 5892
3 Rooms, Double: £80–£90
1 Cottage: £380–£450 weekly
Open: all year, Credit cards: all major
Country House & Self Catering

The King Sitric is Ireland's premier fish restaurant, so here you can enjoy wonderful seafood then be lulled to sleep by the sea just 20 minutes from Dublin airport. Take an aperitif at the long tasting table in the wine cellar while perusing the menu, and then go upstairs to dine in the restaurant with its sweeping views over Dublin Bay. Aidan and Joan explain their food philosophy: "We have built up a network of suppliers of the finest Irish produce. Most of the fish is landed here at Howth. Our smoked salmon is smoked by McLoughlins on the West Pier and crab comes from John Sheridan who fishes Balscadden Bay a stone's throw from our door. Our Irish vegetables and meats are locally produced and mostly organic." After dinner enjoy a gentle stroll down the pier before retiring to bed in rooms named after Irish lighthouses. You'll find lots of polished wood and natural materials with subtle nautical touches. All bedrooms have sea views though Rockabill and Fastnet, the largest rooms at the top of the house, have the best. It's an excellent base for visiting Dublin—a 10-minute walk brings you to the Dart station for a 25-minute ride to Trinity College. Howth marina is just 3-minutes away by foot, while a more energetic hike takes you up to Howth Head. *Directions:* From Dublin airport take the M1 towards Dublin and leave at the first exit, N32, for Malahide Road and Howth. At Howth habor front you will find the King Sitric on your right.

KING SITRIC
Owners: Joan & Aidan MacManus
East Pier
Howth, Co Dublin, Ireland
Tel: 01 832 5235, Fax: 01 839 2442
8 Rooms, Double: €150–€250
Dinner: €55 (not Sun)
Open: all year, Credit cards: all major
Ireland's Blue Book
Restaurant With Rooms

Glenlohane is a lovely Georgian home of spacious but not overly grand rooms, sitting in beautiful, parklike grounds. It is a comfortable house, full of attractive things—lovely antiques and furniture, fires, and rooms in cheerful colors. Hosts Desmond and Melanie—the tenth generation of the family who built the house—are most welcoming, as are their dogs. Enjoy tea by the fire in the drawing room, play a tune on the grand piano, and immerse yourself in the charm of it all. Alternatively, browse through the flowers in the tranquility of the walled garden. For dinner there are two very nice restaurants a five minute drive away in Kanturk. Melanie allows guests to access their email on her computer. Ask about renting the entire house for a week. If renting the main house is not within your pocketbook consider Glenlohane Cottage: a three bedroom, two bath cottage with a large outdoor terrace. Garden lovers are directed to Anne's Grove gardens at Castletownroche and Garinish Island with its grand Italianate gardens. Glenlohane is a working farm of 200 acres with cattle, sheep, horses, and hens; as well as barley, wheat, and oats. *Directions:* From Kanturk take the R576 toward Mallow. Very soon, bear left at the religious monument towards Buttevant on the R580. Take the first right at Sally's Cross towards Ballyclough. Glenlohane is the first residential entrance on the left after 2.5 km—watch for Glenlohane bird sancturary signs the house does not have a sign.

GLENLOHANE
Owners: Melanie & Desmond Sharp Bolster
Kanturk, Co. Cork, Ireland
Tel: 029 50014
4 Rooms, Double: €200
1 Cottage: €750 weekly
Open: all year, Credit cards: all major
Country House & Self Catering

The Irish name for Kenmare, An Neidin, means "the little nest" which is a good description of this attractive town nestling beside the River Kenmare at the foot of some of Ireland's most spectacular scenery. On the Cork road, out of the main bustle of town, The Lodge (purpose-built as a guesthouse and a substantial family home for the Quills and their four young sons) sits back from the road in 2 acres of grassy garden. Finbar works in the family's woollen shop in town, which has the largest selection of sweaters in Kenmare, if not all of Kerry, while Rosemary runs the bed and breakfast. She is exceedingly personable as is her staff of local ladies. Not a thing in the place (with the possible exception of two gigantic vases) is older than the house, from the traditional furniture to the portraits that line the staircase. Bedrooms are spacious and have large, top-of-the-line bathrooms. All have queen-size beds (one a grand four-poster) and nine are large enough to accommodate an additional single bed. One ground-floor bedroom is specially equipped for the handicapped. Kenmare is ideally placed for touring the Ring of Kerry and the prettier Beara Peninsula, as well as for visiting several historic houses and gardens including Muckross House and Derrynane House, home of Daniel O'Connell. *Directions:* Kenmare is about a three-hour drive from Shannon on the N71 between Killarney and Bantry. The Lodge is on the (Cork road) opposite the golf club.

❄ ☕ ✗ 🆑 ☎ P ♿ ⛷ 🏃 🚶 🏇 🚣

THE LODGE
Owners: Rosemary & Finbar Quill
Killowen Road
Kenmare, Co Kerry, Ireland
Tel: 064 41512, Fax: 064 42724
11 Rooms, Double: €100–€120
Open: Mar to Nov, Credit cards: MC, VS
Guesthouse

The Park Hotel has come a long way since it began life in 1897 as the Great Southern Hotel Kenmare to provide a convenient overnight stop for railway travelers en route to or from the Ring of Kerry. Guests are greeted by a blazing coal fire, which casts its glow towards the cozy bar and lounge, and you sit down at a partners' desk to register before being shown to your room. Such touches give a small-hotel feeling to this larger establishment. Exquisite accommodations are provided in nine very luxurious suites with splendid views out over Kenmare Bay. Just as lovely are the superior bedrooms in the old house, many of which have bedrooms and an arch to the seating area—these also all have wonderful views of the bay. Rooms in the "newer" wing have balconies or patios to capture sideways bay views. The restaurant produces some of the finest food that you will find in Ireland. The Park provides programs for the Christmas and New Year holidays. Pamper yourself at the adjacent Sámas spa where you choose from over 40 holistic treatments. Use of the Thermal Suite (sauna, steam, aromatherapy mist and vitality pool with body, foot, and neck massage) is scheduled before your treatment and afterwards you relax on a day bed overlooking the woodlands. The spa has two couples private day suites. Beside the hotel is an 18-hole golf course. *Directions:* Kenmare is about a three-hour drive from Shannon on the N71 between Killarney and Bantry.

THE PARK HOTEL KENMARE
Owner: Francis Brennan
Manager: John Brennan
Kenmare, Co Kerry, Ireland
Tel: 064 41200, Fax: 064 41402
37 Rooms, Double: €498–€606
9 Suites: €696–€846
Dinner: €72
Open: Apr to Oct & Christmas, Credit cards: all major
Ireland's Blue Book
Luxury Resort

Kenmare is one of my favorite Irish towns, and how appropriate that several of my favorite bed and breakfasts are located here, amongst them Sallyport House. Janie Arthur returned home after working for 15 years in California to help her brother, John, convert the family home into a luxurious bed and breakfast, decorating it in an uncluttered, sophisticated style. It's a family affair with John's wife Helen (who runs O'Sullivans pub at nearby Kilmakilogue) and sister Wanie and her children lending a hand. Return in the evening to chat round the fire in the drawing room or curl up in one of the comfortable chairs in the less formal sitting area with its exposed stone wall and old photographs of Kenmare. Breakfast is the only meal served—for dinner, it's a two-minute walk into town. The bedrooms are delightful, each furnished with antiques and accompanied by a large luxurious bathroom. Muxnaw has views of Muxnaw Mountain and deep window seats, Ring View looks out to the River Kenmare, Reen a Gross has an American king-sized four-poster bed, The Falls has a view of the pretty garden. It's delightful to stroll along the riverbank, through the park, and back through the town. You can spend several days exploring the Beara Peninsula, Ring of Kerry, and lakes of Killarney. *Directions:* From Killarney, follow Bantry signposts through Kenmare and Sallyport House is on your left before you come to the bridge.

■ ✄ ☎ @ W P 🚫 🖼 ⛴ 🚶 👣 🏇 ⛵

SALLYPORT HOUSE
Owners: Janie & John Arthur
Kenmare, Co Kerry, Ireland
Tel: 064 42066, Fax: 064 42067
5 Rooms, Double: €140–€175
Open: Apr to Oct, Credit cards: none
B&B

Sea Shore Farm, run by Mary and Owen O'Sullivan, is a particularly peaceful place to stay, no more than five minutes drive from Kenmare or a fifteen minute walk to town by a quiet side road. On arrival you are welcomed with a cup of tea or coffee "to settle you in" and given plenty of information on what to do in and around Kenmare. The lounge, overlooking the Kenmare Bay, has lots of literature on the area. The bedrooms look over the fields across the River Kenmare to the mountains of the Beara Peninsula where the roads are quieter and the scenery very similar to that on the Ring of Kerry. The two downstairs rooms have patios and are wheelchair compatible. It's a blissfully quiet and rural place to stay yet close to the bustle of Kenmare with its excellent restaurants, pubs, and shops. You are just off the Ring of Kerry. If you do not want to deal with coaches and lots of other traffic head for the Beara Peninsula where you get quieter roads and spectacular views. *Directions:* From Kenmare take the Killarney road (N71) for 300 meters. Pass the Esso petrol station on your right and take the next left onto the Ring of Kerry. Sea Shore Farm Guesthouse is signposted to your left after 300 meters.

SEA SHORE FARM GUESTHOUSE
Owners: Mary Patricia & Owen O'Sullivan
Kenmare
Turbrid, Co. Kerry, Ireland
Tel & Fax: 064 41270
6 Rooms, Double: €100–€130
Open: Mar to Nov, Credit cards: MC, VS
Guesthouse

We continue to receive rave reviews on Shelburne Lodge praising not only the high quality of the decor, but also the delicious breakfasts. The building, a Georgian farmhouse, is lovely and the grounds with their lawns, herb garden, and tennis court are very attractive, but it is the interior that is outstanding. The polished wooden floors gleam and lovely antiques grace the sitting room and hallway. Admire Maura's enviable art collection—all by local artists. Each lovely bedroom is accompanied by a luxurious bathroom, each with a different color scheme. Of course, the towel rails are heated and you'll find books of just the sort you want to read and browse through in your room. The same attention to detail goes into the scrumptious breakfast she prepares—even the compote of fresh fruits is artfully garnished. Husband Tom is helpful and friendly, always there with a map and pointing guests in the right direction. Kenmare has some excellent restaurants and Maura as former chef at one of the best (Packies) is happy to make recommendations (advance reservations are a must). Maura also helps her sister Grainne at The Purple Heather, a great venue for lunch or snacks. After dinner wander into one of Kenmare's many pubs—there's entertainment and music to suit all tastes. *Directions:* Shelburne Lodge is on the R569 (Cork road) opposite the golf club.

SHELBURNE LODGE
Owners: Maura & Tom Foley
Kenmare, Co Kerry, Ireland
Tel: 064 41013, Fax: 064 42135
9 Rooms, Double: €120–€175
Open: Mar to mid-Dec, Credit cards: MC, VS
Country House

An impressive tree lined gravel drive leads to Glen house and its gardens, surrounded by three hundred acres of farmland and with sweeping views down to Courtmacsherry Bay and the Atlantic Ocean beyond. Ten generations of the Scott family have farmed the land since the mid 1600's. The house dates back to 1860 but adjacent outbuildings are even older. Current owners Guy and Dianna have renovated and remodeled to provide four extremely comfortable bedrooms and a family suite, three of the rooms have ocean views, all have modern en-suite bathrooms. Guests can relax in front of the fire in the comfortable drawing room or, weather permitting, investigate the walled garden. Diana prides herself on the use of local produce, home grown fruits and vegetables and free range eggs from her own hens. The comprehensive breakfast menu is served on individual tables in the dining room under the watchful stare of John's predecessors, looking down from their framed photographs on the wall. Kinsale, with its shops and restaurants, is just a twenty minute drive away. *Directions:* Located just off the R600 Clonakilty to Kinsale Road. Take the Kilbrittain turnoff from beside the water (there are other Kilbrittain turns) and The Glen is the first house on the left.

THE GLEN
Owners: Diana & Guy Scott
Kilbrittain
Kinsale, Co. Cork, Ireland
Tel & Fax: 023 49862
5 Rooms, Double: €120–€140
1 Suite: €200
Open: Apr to Oct, Credit cards: MC, VS
Country House

A gravel topped driveway curves through the woodland estate towards the early Georgian house, built on what were once the lands of Kilconnell Friary. Current owners the Gossips rescued it from a state of near complete dereliction and have cleverly restored it to its former glory. Paneled walls are painted in bold colors typical of the genre, rooms are tastefully furnished with pictures, antiques and collectibles. An impressive staircase sweeps up from the classic entrance hall to two floors of bedrooms above, the top floor rooms are tucked under the eaves. All have nicely appointed bathrooms en-suite and views over the surrounding countryside. Comfortable beds and crisp linens combine with the secluded surroundings to ensure a restful nights sleep. The comfortably furnished sitting room with black marble fireplace is a great place to curl up with a good book on those occasionally damp days. Breakfast (and dinner by appointment) is served in the blue paneled dining room on the long table in front of the fire and under the stare of one of Suzie's ancestors gazing down from his impressive gilt framed portrait on the wall. *Directions:* From Ballinasloe take the R348 towards Athenry. Pass through Kilconnell village then take the first left towards Capptaggle and immediately left again after 100 meters into an unsignposted lane. Continue past the houses and the lane leads to Ballinderry Park.

BALLINDERRY PARK
Owners: Susie & George Gossip
Kilconnell
Ballinasloe, Co. Galway, Ireland
Tel & Fax: 090 9686796
4 Rooms, Double: €160–€210
Dinner: €55 (not Sun or Mon)
Open: Apr to Oct, Credit cards: MC, VS
Hidden Ireland
Country House

Behind a traditional downtown Kilkenny shopfront sits Zuni (the name of a native American tribe adopted on a whim by Paula), a swish complex of bar, restaurant, and accommodation where ornamentation is kept to a minimum. The narrow bar—the kind where you sip martinis rather than gargle pints of bitter—opens up to the restaurant, where vermilion-red walls contrast with black-and-cream decor and swathes of stainless steel can be seen in the adjacent kitchen. Of course, the food is modern and fun—more Mediterranean than Irish. You find the same modern, minimalist look in the bedrooms, all identically decorated in soft cream with a vermilion-red wall adding a splash of color behind the bed. Beds are heavenly, with crisp white cotton linens and plump duvets. Rooms are by and large snug in size so ask for 101 to 104 or 201 to 204, the larger rooms, or 300, the largest with a queen and two single beds and a big bathroom. Zuni's excellent central location allows you to walk to everything in town. *Directions:* Arriving in Kilkenny from Dublin on the N10, follow signs for City Centre, which bring you down John's Street. Cross the River Nore and you see the castle on your left. Go straight at the traffic lights into Patrick Street and Zuni is on your right after 200 meters. Park in front and collect a map that directs you to nearby parking.

ZUNI
Owners: Paula & Paul Byrne
26 Patrick Street
Kilkenny, Co Kilkenny, Ireland
Tel: 056 7723999, Fax: 056 7756400
13 Rooms, Double: €90–€170
Dinner: from €27.50
Closed: Christmas, Credit cards: all major
Restaurant With Rooms

You would never dream that all the hurly-burly of Killarney town is just down the road when you look out of Coolclogher House to the rolling sheep pastures and distant hills of Killarney. Mary and Maurice Harnett hail from Ireland, and spent a good few years in London where Maurice restored homes in need of complete TLC, a skill he has honed to perfection with Coolclogher House—for the place was a complete disaster when they purchased it. Now it's in perfect condition with each spacious room stylishly decorated. I was especially enchanted by the dining room which opens up to a conservatory with a giant camellia that was a mass of pink blooms. While the Harnetts welcome individual guests on a bed and breakfast basis, do not be disappointed if you cannot secure a reservation for an individual room as they also rent the house on a self-catering basis (sleeps 10-12). When the house is rented the Harnett family decamps to a ground floor two-bedroom apartment. There's not a small room in the place which gives you lots of scope to make yourself comfortable. For dinner guests are directed to the great variety of restaurants in town. Whether viewed from a boat or a pony and trap, the lakes of Killarney are beautiful, but in summer the town can get very crowded. *Directions:* From Killarney take the Muckross road (N71) towards Kenmare. Take first left turn into Mill Road (after metal bridge). Gates on right after 1 km.

COOLCLOGHER HOUSE
Owners: Mary & Maurice Harnett
Mill Road
Killarney, Co. Kerry, Ireland
Tel: 064 35996, Fax: 064 30933
5 Rooms, Double: €240–€295
1 House: €6500 weekly
Open: all year, Credit cards: none
Hidden Ireland
Country House & Self Catering

Killarney is a pleasant town, best to explore after the crowds of daytime visitors have departed. Staying at Earls Court gives you the opportunity to go sightseeing out of town during the day, return in the evening for a cup of tea, and then walk into town for dinner. Emer and Ray built the property and while the exterior is modern, the inside is more traditional, for Emer is a great collector of English and Irish antiques. Guests sign in at reception adjacent to a writing desk once owned by President Cearbhaill O'Dalaigh. Several of the delightful bedrooms have balconies with views of the distant mountains across the trees. Larger rooms have the advantage of spacious sitting areas, king-sized beds and larger bathrooms with a tub and a walk in shower. There's a fully equipped handicap room on the third floor. All bedrooms have delightful antique furniture, (several are four-poster and one an exquisite brass bed), excellent bathrooms with power showers, satellite TV, and phones. Several also have an extra single bed and two bedrooms have an interconnecting door, making them ideal for families. Golfers are spoiled for choice, with Killarney, Waterville, Dooks, Tralee, and Ballybunion the most popular courses, and there's a golf room for clubs. *Directions:* Arriving from Cork on the N22, take a left-hand turn 1 km before the first roundabout in Killarney (or go to the roundabout and retrace your steps). Proceed for 2 km and Earls Court is on your right.

EARLS COURT
Owners: Emer & Ray Moynihan
Woodlawn Junction
Killarney, Co Kerry, Ireland
Tel: 064 34009, Fax: 064 34366
30 Rooms, Double: €125–€195
Open: Mar to mid-Nov, Credit cards: MC, VS
City Hotel

Walk through the front door and you realize the pink façade of the 100 year old building is concealing something different. The lobby, white paneled ceiling, black marble floor, brushed stainless steel trim and luminescent green lighting speaks of a contemporary style more usually found in the chic townhouse hotels of Dublin or Belfast. Inside the trend continues, pink lighting illuminates the dark corridors leading to the guest rooms where muted earth tones are offset with brilliant splashes of color. Modern furnishings, plush bedding and immaculate marble and white bathrooms provide all the creature comforts demanded by today's traveler. All rooms have views across the town or the churchyard. The Lanes cafe bar with its large flat screen TV's is open to the public, a great place to rub shoulders with the locals. A sweeping polished wood and glass staircase leads down to the dining room, "Cellar One". Exposed limestone walls, innovative lighting, wine racks on the wall, and the signature brilliant pink and green upholstery. The shops and restaurants of Killarney are on your doorstep. It's a short walk to Ross Castle or you can take a jaunting car from in front of the hotel. *Directions:* Proceed to Killarney town centre. Park your car at the Killarney Park Hotel and walk across the street to the hotel (next to the church). A porter will collect your luggage.

THE ROSS HOTEL
Owners: Janet & Padraig Treacy
Town Centre
Killarney, Co. Kerry, Ireland
Tel: 064 31855, Fax: 064 27633
27 Rooms, Double: €190–€245
2 Suites: €240–€300
Dinner: €30
Closed: Christmas, Credit cards: all major
City Hotel

Flemingstown House, an 18th-century farmhouse, is just an hour's drive south of Limerick and Shannon airport, a quiet countryside world away from the hustle and bustle. Walk round the farm and chat with Imelda as she works in her spacious kitchen; for the two things that Imelda loves are cooking and taking care of her guests. It would be a shame to stay and not eat, for Imelda prepares tempting meals in which, following the starter and soup, there is a choice of meat or fish as a main course and always three or four desserts and farm cheeses made by her sister and her husband. The intricate stained-glass windows of the conservatory-style dining room were made by the same artist as those in the local church. Upstairs the bedrooms are top of the line, beautifully appointed and provided with a variety of twin and king-size combinations that can accommodate families of all sizes. Each bedroom has a small shower room. Nearby Kilmallock has the ruins of two friaries and the remains of its fortified wall weaving through the town. Guests find this a good base for touring counties Limerick, Tipperary, Kerry, and Cork. *Directions:* From Limerick take the N20 (Cork road) for 30 km and turn left to Kilmallock (10 km). From Kilmallock take the Kilfinane road (R512) for 3 km and the house is on your left.

FLEMINGSTOWN HOUSE
Owner: Imelda Sheedy-King
Kilmallock, Co Limerick, Ireland
Tel: 063 98093, Fax: 063 98546
5 Rooms, Double: €100–€130
Dinner: €45–€50
Open: Feb to Nov, Credit cards: MC, VS
Farmhouse B&B

Maeve Coakley purpose-built this fantastic bed and breakfast set high up over the town. In a place where accommodations are traditional, Maeve's is modern, bright and airy, decorated in utterly peaceful colors. The bedrooms were particularly alluring with their soft-white walls, linen curtains and bedcovers turned down to show Killarney wool blankets, crisp cotton sheets and large square pillows. The largest room is king-bedded with the rest being either queen or twin-bedded. All have immaculate bathrooms with power showers above the tubs, modem sockets, satellite TV, phone, a tea and coffee tray and a trouser press. There's a cozy little sitting room where you can chat by the fire. Breakfast has lots of good things on the menu: fresh fruits and juices, farmhouse cheese and yogurts, organic muesli and hot dishes with smoked salmon and scrambled eggs and catch of the day, as well as the traditional full Irish breakfast. There's several ways to walk into town where you can enjoy views across the sheltered harbor all manner of restaurants and a great many interesting shops. *Directions:* Go straight up the main street in Kinsale (Pearse Street) to the end, turn left and keep going till you see Fishy Fishy restaurant on the right and church on left. Follow the church wall to the left, narrow bend, and Blindgate House is on the left in 400m. There's lots of parking—a real bonus for Kinsale.

BLINDGATE HOUSE
Owner: Maeve Coakley
Blindgate
Kinsale, Co. Cork, Ireland
Tel: 021 4777858, Fax: 021 4777868
11 Rooms, Double: €145–€180
Open: mid-Mar to mid-Dec, Credit cards: all major
B&B

Sitting near the harbor, the Old Bank House occupies a prime heart-of-the-action location in this busy town. At one time these two Georgian townhouses served as a bank and the post office for the community, but now they have achieved a new lease of life as premier accommodation overlooking the sailboat-filled harbor. Here you are at the heart of town, having finally managed to secure a spot for your car on the street. On the ground floor guests have a little sitting area perfect for browsing through the menus from nearby restaurants and toasting their toes on a chilly evening. In the morning enjoy a lavish breakfast before heading out for the day. Bedrooms at the front enjoy the best views and the higher you go, the better the view over the roofs of the town—fortunately there is an elevator. The largest room is the Postmaster's Suite, with a spacious sitting area and fireplace. Beds are twin or king-sized if you request that the twin beds be zipped together. All the rooms have phone, TV, bath with shower over the tub, and Egyptian-cotton towels and bathrobes. The location at the very heart of this most attractive harbor town is ideal: you can stroll round the shops perusing the restaurant menus as you go. *Directions:* Follow the main road into Kinsale (Pearse Street)—the Old Bank House is on the right as you come into town. Parking is on the well-lit street.

OLD BANK HOUSE
Owner: Ciaran Fitzgerald
Pearse Street
Kinsale, Co Cork, Ireland
Tel: 021 4774075, Fax: 021 4774296
16 Rooms, Double: €180–€260
2 Suites: €280–€310
Closed: Christmas, Credit cards: all major
B&B

Beyond the yacht-filled harbor, the narrow streets of Kinsale terrace upwards to high ground. Here you find The Old Presbytery, the home of Noreen and Philip McEvoy who offer a choice of bed and breakfast or self-catering accommodation. The three-bedroom, three-bathroom self-catering apartments offer a sitting room with cheery gas fire in an antique grate, an extra bed that can be pulled down from a wall cupboard, and a kitchenette equipped with light cooking facilities. The Penthouse has a narrow circular staircase going from the living room to the bedrooms where you have views across the rooftops to the harbor (an excellent choice for a party of four). Bed and breakfast guests can choose accommodation that ranges in size from cozy to spacious (a family room with a double and two single beds), with all rooms found up a narrow staircase—leave your large cases in the car. Philip, who used to be a seafood chef, now concentrates his culinary efforts on breakfast, offering everything from traditional Irish fare to crepes filled with fruit in the breakfast room, where an antique Irish pine credenza takes pride of place. *Directions:* Go straight up the main street in Kinsale (Pearse Street) to the end, turn left, first right, and first right, and The Old Presbytery is on the right. Park in the yard.

THE OLD PRESBYTERY
Owners: Noreen & Philip McEvoy
43 Cork Street
Kinsale, Co Cork, Ireland
Tel: 021 4772027, Fax: 021 4772166
3 Rooms, Double: €100–€180
3 Suites: €240–€300
Closed: Dec 1 to Feb 14, Credit cards: MC, VS
B&B & Self Catering

Laura and Andrew Corcoran have given a new lease of life to this grandiose Victorian edifice overlooking the harbor in Kinsale. Previous owners have all implemented their particular visions of grandeur and it is a tribute to the Corcorans' skills that they have consolidated all of the previous changes into a unified whole. A perky fire radiates a welcome in the vast reception hall (plenty of room for all guests to arrive at once) and the sitting and drawing rooms are large enough to provide a seating spot for every guest. Non-public rooms, however, are of more normal proportions. Bedrooms come in all shapes and sizes, from spacious junior suites to snug double rooms. All are attractively decorated in a traditional vein and priced according to their location—how wonderful if they all had harbor views! No matter—you step out the front door onto the harbor and into the heart of this lively town. Our favorite rooms are the four most luxurious tower suites—try to snag room 33 which has French doors opening to its own private courtyard. A buffet breakfast is included in the tariff and there is no shortage of restaurants nearby for dinner. *Directions:* Follow the main road into Kinsale (Long Quay)—Perryville House is on the right just as you come to the harbor. The hotel has several parking spaces opposite the hotel, next to the harbor.

PERRYVILLE HOUSE
Owners: Laura & Andrew Corcoran
Long Quay
Kinsale, Co Cork, Ireland
Tel: 021 4772731, Fax: 021 4772298
22 Rooms, Double: €200–€380
Open: Apr to Oct, Credit cards: MC, VS
B&B

Visitors will truly appreciate the central location of The Pier House. This boutique B&B stands in its own secluded garden, a mere few steps from the harbor, restaurants, shops, and lively pubs of Kinsale. The house has a crisp air of contemporary upscale elegance. Its rooms are bright and airy, with dark wide plank floors offset by walls painted in fresh white and adorned with paintings by a local artist. The accent colors are taupe and burgundy. Goose-down comforters and immaculate white linens adorn the sleigh beds. The en-suite bathrooms have gray slate floors, black counters, gleaming white fixtures, spacious walk-in showers, and feature toiletries by Gilcrist and Soames. Three of the second-floor rooms have small balconies with harbor views. Those desiring some extra relaxation will find a sauna on an outdoor private deck. A sumptuous breakfast is graciously served and many will appreciate the privacy of individual tables. Long-time residents Ann and Pat Hagerty are more than willing to offer advice on where to dine and how to spend your time in Kinsale and the surrounding area. The Pier House has two entrances: one on the harbor side and another from Main Street, a side avenue filled with colorful eateries and shops. *Directions:* Coming from Cork arrive at the Kinsale waterfront with SuperValu on your right, turn left, next left at the tourist office and Pier House is on your right, opposite the carpark.

PIER HOUSE
Owners: Ann & Pat Hegarty
Pier House
Pier Road
Kinsale, Co. Cork, Ireland
Tel & Fax: 021 4774475
10 Rooms, Double: €120–€160
Closed: Christmas, Credit cards: MC, VS
B&B

On the next bay down the coast from the Cliffs of Moher Moy House, a lovely hotel caressed by wispy breezes rising off the sea, has waves lapping at the bottom of the garden. Built as a stylish holiday home in the early 1800s, the property has undergone a complete transformation with all but three bedrooms having superb sea views—several have window seats in the bedroom and the bathroom. Relax with a drink from the honesty bar in the chic drawing room and contemplate the delectable offerings on the menu before going down the narrow spiral staircase to the conservatory dining room. Locally produced produce enhances the dining experience. Downstairs bedrooms Kilmaheen and Kilfarboy are particularly spacious and have large bathrooms, with separate bathtubs and showers. Upstairs, Moymore is a favorite with lots of room and a window seat in its bay window. For the most spectacular view, clamber up the narrow stairs that take you to the top of the tower. At low tide wander along the quiet beach and round the headland to the bustling little holiday town of Lahinch. While golfers head for the popular Lahinch golf course, sightseers drive along the coast. Visit the Cliffs of Moher and The Burren. *Directions:* From Ennis take the N85 through Ennistymon to Lahinch. Go up the main street and take the first left, then turn left again following signposts for Miltown Malbay. After 2 km the entrance to Moy House is on the right.

MOY HOUSE
General Manager: Brid O'Meara
Lahinch, Co Clare, Ireland
Tel: 065 7082800, Fax: 065 7082500
9 Rooms, Double: €195–€290
2 Suites: €250–€390
Dinner: €55
Closed: Jan to mid-Feb, Credit cards: all major
Ireland's Blue Book
Country House Hotel

Delphi Lodge with its surrounding estate was for centuries the sporting estate of the Marquis of Sligo. This wild, unspoilt, and beautiful valley with its towering mountains, tumbling rivers, and crystal-clear loughs was acquired in 1986 by Jane and Peter Mantle. Fortunately for those who have a love of wild, beautiful places, they have restored the Marquis' fishing lodge and opened their home to guests who come to walk, fish for salmon, relax, and enjoy the camaraderie of the house-party atmosphere. In the evening Peter often presides at the head of the very long dinner table (guests who catch a salmon take the place of honor) where guests enjoy a leisurely meal and lively conversation. A snug library and an attractive drawing room are at hand and guests often spend late-night hours in the billiard room. Bedrooms are all furnished in antique and contemporary pine. On a recent visit we especially admired rooms 3 and 4, two larger rooms with spacious bathrooms and fabulous views of the lake. Such is the popularity of the place that it is advisable to make reservations well in advance to secure a summer booking. Five deluxe, self-catering cottages are also available on the estate. *Directions:* Leenane is between Westport and Clifden on the N59. From Leenane go east towards Westport for 3 km, turn left, and continue along the north shore of Killary harbor towards Louisburgh for 8 km. Delphi Lodge is in the woods, on the left after the adventure center.

DELPHI LODGE
Owners: Jane & Peter Mantle
Leenane
Delphi, Co. Galway, Ireland
Tel: 095 42222, Fax: 095 42296
12 Rooms, Double: €200–€270
5 Cottages: €600–€1250 weekly
Dinner: €50
Open: mid-Jan to mid-Dec, Credit cards: MC, VS
Hidden Ireland
Country House & Self Catering

Rosleague Manor is a lovely Irish hotel—a comfortable country house hotel overlooking Ballinakill Bay and an ever-changing panorama of wild Connemara countryside. This is a quiet, sparsely populated land of steep hills, tranquil lakes, and grazing sheep, where narrow country lanes lead to little hamlets. Manager Mark Foyle is much in evidence, making certain that guests are well taken care of. The hotel is beautifully furnished with lovely old furniture, and the sitting rooms are cozy with their turf fires and comfortable chairs. The garden-style conservatory is a popular place for before- or after-dinner drinks. Bedrooms are most attractive, my preference being for those with views across the gardens to the sea and distant hills. Two particularly lovely ground floor rooms are perfect for those who have difficulty with stairs. The dining room is my favorite room in the house: tall windows frame the view and lovely old tables and chairs are arranged in groupings. There is an à-la-carte menu as well as the fixed-price menu that offers four or five choices for each course. Dishes vary with the seasons and include a wide selection of locally caught fish and Connemara lamb. This is a peaceful place to hide away and a well-located base for exploring the ruggedly beautiful countryside of Connemara. *Directions:* Take the N59 from Galway to Clifden then turn right at the church for the 10-km drive to Rosleague Manor.

ROSLEAGUE MANOR
Manager: Mark Foyle
Letterfrack
Connemara, Co. Galway, Ireland
Tel: 095 41101, Fax: 095 41168
16 Rooms, Double: €160–€220
4 Suites: €190–€250
Dinner: €50
Open: Easter to Nov, Credit cards: all major
Ireland's Blue Book
Country House Hotel

One of the joys of coming to stay with Beryl and James is that you get to see the completion of their various projects, first the house, then acres of gardens—the Japanese and French gardens, the conversion of the stables to a restaurant and the addition of seven spacious suites with a living room on the ground floor and bedroom above. The imposing house was built in the 1740s for the Cuffe family and was later the residence of the land agent who oversaw the Earl of Longford's estates. The upstairs drawing room boasts specially commissioned chandeliers and period furniture. Also on the first floor is a particular favorite, a very spacious suite which has a sitting room with open fire and a spacious bathroom. On the top floor Purple is the room to request not only for its vibrant color but also for its spaciousness. Breakfast is served at small tables in the ground-floor breakfast room with its beautiful fan-vaulted ceilings. Viewmount House is an ideal base for trips to Clonmacnoise, Birr Castle, and Newgrange. Garden enthusiasts head for Strokestown House with its 6 acres of gardens and Tullynally Castle with its Chinese and Tibetan Gardens. Longford's golf course is just across the back fence. *Directions:* Coming from the south, leave the N4 (Dublin to Sligo road) at the first roundabout in Longford towards Longford town. After the speed limit sign you see Viewmount House's sign. Turn very sharp left and the house is on your right in 500 meters.

VIEWMOUNT HOUSE
Owners: Beryl & James Kearney
Dublin Road
Longford, Co Longford, Ireland
Tel: 043 41919, Fax: 043 42906
13 Rooms, Double: €160–€250
Dinner: €55
Open: all year, Credit cards: all major
B&B

Kilkenny is a most attractive, historic town, and there is no more perfect a base for exploring its many charms than Blanchville House, a 15-minute drive away. Acres of farmland give this handsome Georgian home seclusion. You'll know you've arrived when you see a tall, square, church tower-like folly. Inside Blanchville House, tall-ceilinged, generously proportioned rooms are the order of the day, and Monica has several pieces of furniture that were made for the house. One of these is the half-tester bed that graces the principal bedroom. Apparently Sir James Kearny, a great eccentric, was fond of waxing and singeing his mustache, an operation he performed in his bed. One day, while practicing this routine, he set fire to the bedding and narrowly escaped burning the house down. There's a portrait of Sir James in the drawing room, which has the wallpaper hung in 1823: guests enjoy a drink here before going in to dine together round the long polished table. Three lovely self-catering cottages (one handicap friendly) are found in the old stables and gardener's cottage (sleeps 3 to 6). *Directions:* Leave Kilkenny on the N10 (Carlow/Dublin road) in the direction of Dublin. Take the first right 1 km after The Pike pub, 6 km out. Continue over railway crossing following signs to Denbell. Turn left the first crossrods, Connolly's pub, and the first large stone house on your left after 2 km. There is no village of Maddoxtown and Dunbell is Connolly's pub.

BLANCHVILLE HOUSE
Owners: Monica & Tim Phelan
Dunbell
Maddoxtown, Co. Kilkenny, Ireland
Tel: 056 7727197, Fax: 056 7727636
6 Rooms, Double: €120–€130
3 Cottages: €350–€650 weekly
Dinner: €45 (not Sun or Mon)
Open: Mar to Nov, Credit cards: all major
Hidden Ireland
Country House & Self Catering

Set back from the road in its own gardens and surrounded by green fields Newforge House is an oasis of calm scarcely thirty minutes drive from Belfast and both of its airports. Built in the late 1700's by a successful linen merchant, (remnants of his mill are still standing at the back of the property) the house has been in the family of its current owners for six generations. It was lovingly restored and renovated over a two year period by John and Louise Mathers and opened to receive guests in 2005. Food is a major focus, local produce is sourced and prepared personally by John. Comfortably proportioned sitting and dining rooms are beautifully furnished, collectibles and modern furniture blend with carefully restored architectural features; plaster cornices, wooden window shutters, marble and black iron fireplaces. Bedrooms, named after various ladies in the family history, are to be found on the second and third floors. I particularly liked the four poster and half tester beds in the superior rooms. Standard rooms on the third floor, while a trifle simpler and with slightly lower ceiling are also very lovely. All are provided with elegant en-suite bathrooms. Visiting the Giants Causeway makes a great day out while closer at hand are Belfast and an array of interesting houses and gardens. *Directions:* Leave the M1 West at exit 9 signpost Moira A3. After 5km, in Magheralin, turn left at Byrne's pub and the house is on your left after the speed limit sign.

NEWFORGE HOUSE
Owners: Lou & John Mathers
58 Newforge Road
Magheralin, BT67 0QL, Northern Ireland
Tel: 028 9261 1255, Fax: 028 9261 2823
6 Rooms, Double: £110–£165
Dinner: £32.50 (not Sun or Mon)
Closed: Christmas & New Year, Credit cards: MC, VS
Ireland's Blue Book
Country House

The sheer size of Longueville House takes your breath away. Set on a hill overlooking the River Blackwater, this wonderful country house offers you the very best of Irish hospitality. It was built by Richard Longfield, who was spurred on to grander things by a sum of money he received for supporting the British Act of Union. The house is now owned by the O'Callaghan family whose forebears had the estate confiscated from them by Cromwell in 1650. The O'Callaghans take great pains to make sure that you enjoy your stay: Aisling makes certain you are well cared for and made to feel completely at home while William ensures that you are well fed. Longueville is almost completely self-sufficient with vegetables, salmon, lamb, and herbs coming from the estate. The dining room in soft shades of pink is a picture and extends into the Victorian conservatory (1862), while the adjacent library provides a snug place to dine. Each and every bedroom is beautifully decorated and accompanied by a splendid modern bathroom. Reservations can be made for salmon and trout fishing on the nearby Blackwater. There are several 18-hole golf courses within easy reach of Longueville. *Directions:* The hotel is located on the N72, 5 km west of Mallow on the Killarney road.

LONGUEVILLE HOUSE
Owners: Aisling & William O'Callaghan
Mallow, Co Cork, Ireland
Tel: 022 47156, Fax: 022 47459
20 Rooms, Double: €230–€280
3 Suites: €300–€380
Dinner: €65
Closed: Jan 7 to Mar 15, Credit cards: all major
Ireland's Blue Book
Country House Hotel

The 5-foot-thick wall in the dining room, the stone arch that leads to the kitchen, and the ancient defense wall in the garden are remnants of the 15th century keep that stood atop this rocky promontory. It's a "home" that has been added to over the years—a good bit of the house is over 300 years old with the most recent addition being shower rooms for each guest room. Beds are large and rooms are most attractively decked out. My favorite bedrooms were Lady Mary's room with its big bay window looking across the garden wall to miles of countryside and Deedee Walsh, a spacious room at the back. Joan and her daughter Catherine are the most welcoming and attentive of hostesses. They strongly believe in keeping you well fed: breakfasts have to be seen to be believed—a vast array of fruit dishes alongside fresh scones and a variety of hot dishes. Scones and a pot of tea (sometimes homemade pie) are served in the afternoon to keep you going between lunch and dinner. It's a delightful spot just a few minutes from the main roads that whisk you into Waterford and Cork. There are some lovely drives in this area (The Vee and Nire Valley to Clonmel) and several castles (Cahir and Lismore), and the sea with Dungarvan and Youghal is just over the hills. *Directions:* From Dungarven take the N72 towards Cork for 9.5 km (after Cappagh) and turn right on the R761 signposted Clonmel. After 5 km turn right in Millstreet, cross the bridge and the property is on your right.

CASTLE COUNTRY HOUSE
Owners: Joan & Emmett Nugent
Millstreet
Cappagh, Co. Waterford, Ireland
Tel: 058 68049
5 Rooms, Double: €90–€110
Dinner: €30
Open: Mar to Nov, Credit cards: MC, VS
Farmhouse B&B

Amongst the scattered modern holiday cottages surrounding the village of Miltown Malbay, a popular Irish holiday destination; you find a traditional Irish farmhouse that is now a welcoming guesthouse, restaurant, and cookery school operated by Rita Meade. Rita offers cookery courses for adults, teenagers, and children. The heart of the house is the country kitchen with its large central island designed for cooking classes. There are comfortable chairs in the sitting room with its old country dresser. The adjacent dining room has been extended with a sunny conservatory. Dinner has four to five choices in each of the three courses. The country theme is continued in the bedrooms with their pine furniture and old beds topped with quilts. All bedrooms have televisions and compact shower rooms and three rooms have a double and a single bed. There is a small ground-floor double-bedded room for those who have difficulty with stairs. The nearby Cliffs of Moher are a great attraction but you can use Berry Lodge as a base for visiting Bunratty Folk Park, Craggaunowen Megalithic Centre, the Aran Islands, exploring The Burren, and sailing to Scattery Island. *Directions:* From Ennis (on the Limerick to Galway road) take the N85 to Inagh then the R460 to Miltown Malbay (32 km total). Take the N67 Spanish Point Road in the center of the village, pass the caravan park, cross the bridge, take the second left, and Berry Lodge is first on the right.

BERRY LODGE
Owner: Rita Meade
Miltown Malbay
Annagh, Co. Clare, Ireland
Tel: 065 7087022, Fax: 065 7087011
5 Rooms, Double: €90–€96
Dinner: €40
Closed: mid-Jan to mid-Feb, Credit cards: MC, VS
B&B

Lough Owel Lodge is a modern house set between Lough Owel and a quiet country road that runs into Mullingar. While the house has no architectural distinction, this is a tranquil country spot where you can cycle down quiet roads, stroll the shores of Lough Owel, and generally enjoy the peace and quiet of the center of Ireland. Aideen and Martin Ginnell find that the house works really well for raising a family of four children and providing bed and breakfast; for it is divided into two parts, the front being for guests and the back for their family. I particularly appreciated the large car port which sheltered me from the rain as I arrived. A large sitting room with comfortable sofas and floor-to-ceiling windows offering views of the garden and lake adjoins the dining room with its lovely old table and chairs. Upstairs, the two premier rooms are Lough Ennell with its king-sized, four-poster bed and Lough Owel with its family heirloom mahogany half-tester double bed. A family suite consists of a small double bedroom leading to a small twin-bedded room and a bathroom. Guests often wander down to the lough, enjoy a game of tennis, and make use of the children's game room. Tullynally Castle, Carrickglass Manor, Belvedere House, Fore Abbey, and Athlone Castle are within an hour's drive. *Directions:* Take the N4 from Dublin towards Sligo. After passing the third exit for Mullingar, Lough Owel Lodge is signed to your left after 1 km.

LOUGH OWEL LODGE
Owners: Aideen & Martin Ginnell
Mullingar
Cullion, Co. Westmeath, Ireland
Tel: 044 9348714
5 Rooms, Double: €80–€90
Open: Apr to Oct, Credit cards: MC, VS
B&B

Readers' letters praise the warmth of welcome, the delectable food, the quality and utter charm of this country house—and the fact that Mornington is an hour and a half's drive from Dublin airport, making it an ideal first or last destination in Ireland. I totally concur; for a stay at Mornington House with Anne and Warwick, the fifth generation of his family to call this home, is also something I find completely delightful. The O'Haras have an easy way of making guests feel at home. They chat with them in the drawing room after dinner, and put a lot of trouble into helping them with their activities and sightseeing in this unspoiled region with its lakes, canals, and gently undulating countryside. Anne is a talented cook, producing delicious dinners and outstanding breakfasts. Families are welcome and children can be served an early tea. The two front bedrooms are enormous: one has a large brass bed sitting center stage while the other has a Victorian double bed and shares the view across the peaceful grounds. The third bedroom, a delightful twin-bedded room, looks out to the side garden and the woods. The oldest wing of the house contains two smaller bedrooms overlooking the kitchen garden. *Directions:* From Dublin take the Sligo Road to the Mullingar bypass. Exit for Castlepollard and go 10 km to Crookedwood, where you turn left by The Wood pub. After 2 km turn right and Mornington is on your right after 1 km.

MORNINGTON HOUSE
Owners: Anne & Warwick O'Hara
Mullingar
Mornington-Multyfarnham, Co. Westmeath, Ireland
Tel: 044 9372191, Fax: 044 9372338
5 Rooms, Double: €150
Dinner: €45
Open: Apr to Oct, Credit cards: all major
Hidden Ireland
Country House

A mere stone's throw from Galway Bay, Mount Vernon was built in the late eighteenth century as a residence for Colonel William Persse of Roxborough. In spite of serving on the "wrong" side in the American War of Independence, he became a friend of George Washington with whom he shared an interest in plants and gardens. The walled garden contains Cypress trees thought to have been a gift from the American President. The house eventually came to Lady Augusta Gregory, Persse's great-granddaughter and an avid supporter of the arts. During her tenure, she entertained such luminaries as W.B. Yeats, George Russel and George Bernard Shaw. The house contains several architectural features, fireplaces, an Arts and Craft staircase, Batiks and painted panels of that era. Current owners Mark Helmore and Ally Raftery have caringly renovated and extended the house to include five very smart bedrooms featuring antique furniture and stylish collectibles from their world travels. Go to Doolin to catch a boat to view the Cliffs of Moher or head for Kilfenora to learn all about the Burren landscape. *Directions:* Leave the N18 at Kilcolgan and follow the N67 through Kinvarra and continue on the cost road for 6km. Turn right across the middle of a small lake signpost Linnane's Lobster Bar. Turn left at the lobster bar and right at the art gallery, proceed along the shore and Mount Vernon is the fourth house on your left.

MOUNT VERNON
Owners: Ally Raftery & Mark Helmore
New Quay, Co. Clare, Ireland
Tel: 065 7078126, Fax: 065 7078118
5 Rooms, Double: €220
Dinner: €55 (not Mon or Tue)
Open: Apr to Dec, Credit cards: MC, VS
Hidden Ireland
Country House

The O'Donnell family's picturesque farmhouse has great appeal. It is over 200 years old and has received a sensitive restoration. There's a snug little lounge with a low thick stone arch that was one of the original doors in the house attesting to the fact that folks must have been much smaller in days gone by. A bay window nook overlooks the front garden and provides a perfect place for laying out your map and planning the days activities, returning home for one of Ber's excellent home-cooked dinners. Upstairs there are three guest bedrooms: 1: a tiny double with en suite shower (usually rented as a single), 2: a snug twin with bathroom, and 3: a larger room with zip-link beds with an en suite shower room. Take a stroll round the lovely garden and walk down to and along the riverbank. Trout fishing is a great draw. Walkers head for the hills—Kilmaneen is surrounded by the Comeraghs, Knockmealdowns, and Galtee Mountains. Kevin can either take you out for the day in a group walking or supply you with maps. Sightseers have lots to keep them busy with driving The Vee and visiting Lismore, Cahir, Cappoquin, and Swiss Cottage. If you have a family, enquire about renting the adjacent little two-bedroom cottage, either for bed and breakfast or on a self-catering basis. *Directions:* Go through Newcastle, towards Cloheen, at the Y-junction bear right down a narrow, winding lane, and Kilmaneen is on your right after 2 km.

KILMANEEN FARMHOUSE
Owners: Bernadette & Kevin O'Donnell
Newcastle
Clonmel, Co. Tipperary, Ireland
Tel: 052 36231
3 Rooms, Double: €90–€95
Dinner: €30 (not Sun)
Open: Apr to Dec, Credit cards: MC, VS
Farmhouse B&B & Self Catering

When Lord Inchiquin sold Dromoland Castle in 1963, he moved five minutes up the hill to Thomond House, a large Georgian-style mansion. Now it is home to his nephew Conor O'Brien (the present Lord Inchiquin and head of the O'Brien chieftancy) and his family—and what a delightful home it is, with its high-ceilinged rooms looking out through tall windows to the surrounding countryside. An air of quiet formality is the order of the day. Guests enjoy a comfortable drawing room, take breakfast in the dining room, and watch television in the library. A sweeping staircase leads to the upper gallery and bedrooms, which are beautifully outfitted and offer views of the parkland or the adjacent castle. Two additional lovely bedrooms are found in a ground floor wing. You might want to walk down to Dromoland Castle for a superbly formal meal or drive a few kilometers further to less expensive restaurants. Guests often play golf on the neighboring course or roam over the estate, while farther afield lies the Burren, Lahinch, Doonbeg and Ballybunion golf courses. It's a perfect first or last destination in Ireland if you are flying in or out of Shannon airport. *Directions:* From Shannon Airport take the N18 towards Ennis. Exit signpost Quin and Ballygirran (not Newmarket on Fergus) and take the Dromoland exit from the roundabout. After 1km, at the end of the Dromoland Castle wall, turn left into Thomond House's driveway.

THOMOND HOUSE
Owners: Helen & Conor Inchiquin
Newmarket-on-Fergus, Co Clare, Ireland
Tel: 061 368304, Fax: 061 368285
5 Rooms, Double: €240–€400
Closed: Christmas, Credit cards: all major
Country House

Built on a sheltered site with distant views across Strangford Lough to the Mourne Mountains, Edenvale House is the lovely home of a most gregarious couple, Diane and Gordon Whyte. Relax with tea and cakes in the beautiful drawing room, plan your sightseeing forays, and enjoy the complete tranquility of this lovely spot. Try to snag one of the spacious front bedrooms with their spectacular views; dressing rooms large enough to accommodate a bed for a child, and spacious bathrooms with both bath and shower. (One's a queen-size four-poster, the other a king or twin.) The two other very lovely bedrooms have garden views and spacious shower rooms. There's a beautiful garden to wander in and horses and ponies to enjoy. Just down the road, Mount Stewart House has a splendid interior and a painting by Stubbs, but the acres of magnificent gardens are the main attraction. Nearby, the village of Greyabbey has lots of antique shops and the ruins of a Cistercian abbey. Dozens of old buildings have been brought from the countryside to the Ulster Folk Park where demonstrations of traditional crafts and farming are given. *Directions:* From Belfast take the A20 through Newtownards in the direction of Portaferry. After 3.2 km the entrance to Edenvale House is on the left.

EDENVALE HOUSE
Owners: Diane & Gordon Whyte
130 Portaferry Road
Newtownards, BT22 2AH, Northern Ireland
Tel: 028 9181 4881
4 Rooms, Double: £80–£90
Closed: Christmas, Credit cards: MC, VS
Country House

Eoin's great-great-grandfather came to the Nire Valley to build the church. He married a local girl Hanora and together they lived in a little cottage adjacent to the church nestled beside the tumbling River Nire in this delightfully wild and isolated spot on the edge of the Comeragh Mountains. They would not recognize their little home for it has been extended to include a parade of sitting rooms, spacious restaurant, hot tub for eight in the conservatory, and array of large bedrooms. All bedrooms have Jacuzzi bathtubs—just for fun, reserve one of the six rooms whose bathrooms come equipped with Jacuzzi tubs for two. Whenever you come to stay, you can be sure of being well fed—Mary, Eoin's mum, lays out a feast of a breakfast for which there is always a variety of freshly baked breads. In the evening Eoin (pronounced Owen) and his wife Judith offer a set, four-course, dinner with lots of choices for starters and main courses. Packed lunches, maps, and directions are available for walks that range from leisurely rambles to challenging hill hikes. Non-walkers can drive to Lismore, Cashel, or over The Vee, returning in time for a visit to one of the nearby pubs for a drink and perhaps (more often in the summer months) a late-night Irish music session. *Directions:* From Clonmel or Dungarvan, follow the R672 as far as Ballymacarbry, where you turn left at Melody's Lounge Bar. Travel 5.6 km and Hanora's is beside the church just before the stone bridge.

HANORA'S COTTAGE GUESTHOUSE
Owners: Mary, Judith & Eoin Wall
Nire Valley
Clonmel, Co. Waterford, Ireland
Tel: 052 36134, Fax: 052 36540
10 Rooms, Double: €190–€250
Dinner: €50
Closed: Christmas, Credit cards: MC, VS
Guesthouse

Guests at Currarevagh House (pronounced "Curra-reeva") find themselves entering a world reminiscent of the turn of the last century. Tranquility reigns supreme and things are done the good old-fashioned way at Currarevagh House. However, do not be afraid that you will be deprived of central heating and private bathrooms, for this is not the case. If you book well in advance, you may be able to secure one of our four favorite rooms (1, 2, or 3 in the main house, or room 16 in the "new" wing with its lake views). There are several smaller rooms in the new wing. Try to arrive by 4:30 pm when tea and cakes are served—you will then have enough time for a brisk woodland or lakeshore walk to make room for a delicious dinner at 8. A gong announces dinner and while there are no choices, the helpings are of generous proportions. A tempting breakfast buffet of cold meats, cheeses, and traditional cooked breakfast dishes is spread on the sideboard and the hotel is happy to pack you a picnic lunch for your day's excursion. It's all very old-fashioned and un-decorator-perfect, but you will thoroughly enjoy it. Harry can arrange for fishing on the adjacent Lough Corrib. The gardens fringed by rhododendrons and hydrangeas have a croquet lawn and lovely views across Lough Corrib the second largest lake in Ireland. *Directions:* From Galway take the N59 to Oughterard, turn right in the center of the village, and follow the lake shore for the 6-km drive to the house.

CURRAREVAGH HOUSE
Owners: June & Harry Hodgson
Oughterard
Connemara, Co. Galway, Ireland
Tel: 091 552312, Fax: 091 552731
13 Rooms, Double: €160–€220
Dinner: €48
Open: Apr to mid-Oct, Credit cards: MC, VS
Ireland's Blue Book
Country House Hotel

Carmel is the sixth generation of her family to live in the Oughterard area and the first to be more interested in interior design than the Connemara ponies that her family has always raised. Named Railway Lodge because it stands adjacent to a former railway line—now a walking path—the house has a modern exterior and country style interior. There's a snug parlor with a fire and a sunny conservatory overlooking the rolling gorse and distant mountains. Stylish bedrooms have queen-sized beds with crisp white sheets and duvets, and antique pine furniture—each with a top-of-the-line shower room. For dinner we walked the ten minutes into Oughterard and Carmel lent us a flashlight to guide us home. Breakfast proved to be a sumptuous affair. The offer of fresh-baked scones and bread and poached fruit led us to decline the offer of a cooked breakfast. If you would like to stay for a week Carmel has a lovely one bedroom cottage in the garden. If you have an interest in walking, local history or Connemara ponies, Carmel refers you to her father who lives nearby. Lough Corrib is a popular fishing venue. Non-fisher types enjoy spectacular drives through rugged countryside and trips to islands on the lough. *Directions:* Arriving in Oughterard from Galway you see the Corrib Hotel on the left, turn left beside it and then immediate right (do not go straight). Continue to fork in road and take a right and Railway Lodge is the 2nd entrance on the left.

RAILWAY LODGE
Owners: Carmel Geoghegan & Joe Howlett
Canrower
Oughterard, Co. Galway, Ireland
Tel: 091 552945
5 Rooms, Double: €100–€110
1 Cottage: €650 weekly
Open: all year, Credit cards: MC, VS
Hotel & Self Catering

Portlaoise has been bypassed with a new road and you can once again enjoy the quiet in this heart-of-Ireland town. Situated close to downtown on a side street, Ivyleigh House is set back from the road, its immaculate Georgian façade heralds a first-class interior furnished and decorated in a delightful traditional style. A lovely sitting room is available for guests' use and for breakfast there's a handsome dining room, its large communal table decked out with china and crystal. Dinah does an excellent breakfast with the freshest of local ingredients including free-range eggs, local bacon, and natural yogurt with geranium jelly. Then there's perfect porridge with cream, homemade brown bread, tea made with leaf tea, and freshly brewed coffee. The spacious bedrooms are particularly comfortable with top-of-the-line beds, linen sheets and pillowcases, and large shower rooms with power showers. One is located downstairs on the garden level. There is no shortage of restaurants for dinner. Portlaoise is well placed for visiting Tullamore, Kildare, Kilkenny, and Carlow, the Slieve Bloom Mountains, Emo Court, and the Rock of Dunamase, an ancient fort. A 2 bedroom cottage at Killenard is available for weekly rental. *Directions:* Approaching from Cork, turn off the N8 for Portlaoise. In Portlaoise drive straight through two roundabouts onto the N80 for 30 meters, turn right at the railway bridge, and Ivyleigh House is the second house on the left.

IVYLEIGH HOUSE
Owners: Dinah & Jerry Campion
Bank Place, Church Street
Portlaoise, Co. Laois, Ireland
Tel: 057 8622081, Fax: 057 8663343
6 Rooms, Double: €125–€150
1 Cottage: €800–€900 weekly
Closed: Dec 23 to Jan 2, Credit cards: MC, VS
Guesthouse & Self Catering

Ardeen country house is situated in the heritage town of Ramelton overlooking the River Lennon. This Victorian house gives you a homey relaxed feeling the moment you walk through the front door. Ardeen is the onetime home of Nurse Black who was the private nurse to King George V. The book King's Nurse, Beggar's Nurse tells her story. Anne and Bert Campbell have been welcoming guests into their lovely home for many years. Anne enjoys baking and will spoil you with afternoon tea and home made scones as soon as you arrive. Breakfast is served around the beautiful antique dining table and includes fresh fruits, home made brown bread and scones as well as the traditional Irish breakfast. The bedrooms are all very nicely furnished and individually decorated and in keeping with the house. Four are en suite and a twin room enjoys a large private bathroom. The adjacent stable has been converted to a snug holiday cottage with an exposed stone living room, attractive kitchen and three bedrooms, one of which is en suite. Ardeen is an ideal base for exploring the Donegal coastline and visiting Glenveagh National Park and the Glebe Art Gallery with its fine collection of Irish paintings. *Directions:* If you are arriving from Donegal, take the N56 to Letterkenny and on the outskirts of the town look for the T72, signposted for Rathmullen. It's an 11-km drive to Ramelton. When you reach the river turn right, following the bank, and Ardeen is on your right.

ARDEEN
Owners: Anne & Bert Campbell
Ramelton, Co Donegal, Ireland
Tel & Fax: 074 91 51243
5 Rooms, Double: €90
1 Cottage: €350–€550 weekly
Open: Easter to Oct, Credit cards: MC, VS
B&B & Self Catering

Frewin was a rectory for over 150 years and its earlier fortified annex dates back to the 1600s. Thomas, a restorer of old homes, antique collector, and raiser of rare-breed animals, found a family link while he was refurbishing the house: his great-aunt Susan had written her name on the back of one of the cupboards in the maid's room in 1912. If you do not mind having your own private shower room down the hall, you can stay in Aunt Susan's room. The other three bedrooms are small suites with sitting room areas—one has a claw-foot tub in the bathroom and the other two have showers. Our favorite, the green room, has a king-sized bedroom and, through the shower room, a private library which can double as a sitting room. There's lots of interesting furniture (a praying wall and sideboard from Glenveagh Castle) and pictures (the library is covered with old Vanity Fair prints). Regina and Thomas are hospitable and easygoing. Several of Thomas's finds are for sale in a little courtyard store. If you want to stay for a week, there are two little cottages tucked into quiet corners of the 2-acre garden. Ramelton is a 17th-century town with handsome houses and old riverside warehouses. A scenic route winds up Fanad Peninsula to Rathmullan and Portsalon. *Directions:* From Letterkenny take R245 towards Ramelton. Travel 11 km, pass the Shell station (on right), continue 800 meters and turn right at speed limit sign—Frewin is 400 meters along on the right.

FREWIN
Owners: Regina & Thomas Coyle
Ramelton, Co Donegal, Ireland
Tel & Fax: 074 9151246
4 Rooms, Double: €130–€180
1 Cottage: €450–€550 weekly
Dinner: €50
Closed: Christmas, Credit cards: MC, VS
Hidden Ireland
Country House & Self Catering

Rathmullan House has the most tranquil setting amidst mature trees and rose gardens that slope down to a sandy beach, with views of the mountains across Lough Swilly. The second generation of the Wheeler family run the hotel creating a relaxing and friendly atmophere. It's a delightfully rambling house with large sitting rooms (one in an Indian Raj style) leading to Batt's bar presided over by the portrait of Mrs. Batt who had Rathmullan house built as her summer home in the 1800s. Here you can enjoy drinks and lighter fare. Three-or four-course dinners are served in the dining room where meters of fabric are gathered into peaks dotted with fairy lights to create softest of lighting and the most romantic of dining atmospheres. Bedrooms are either "view" (garden and lough) or "not" and fall into three categories: Regency; (delectable, subtly themed, oh-so-spacious rooms with terrace or balcony and grand bathrooms of which the two penthouses offer the ultimate in luxury); Balcony (spacious rooms with top of the line bathrooms, terrace or balcony); or Main House (mainly high-ceilinged rooms divided between no view and lough view rooms—try to snag one with a spacious bay-window). Enjoy a walk on the beach, a swim in the pool, a game of tennis or a relaxing massage in the Solace room. *Directions:* From Letterkenny take the R245 through Ramelton and Rathmullan. The hotel is on the right as you pass the Catholic church upon leaving the village.

RATHMULLAN HOUSE
Owners: Mary, Mark, Yvonne & William Wheeler
Rathmullan
Letterkenny, Co. Donegal, Ireland
Tel: 074 9158188, Fax: 074 9158200
32 Rooms, Double: €170–€330*
*Service: 10%
Dinner: €55
Open: all year, Credit cards: all major
Ireland's Blue Book
Country House Hotel

Hunter's Hotel has adopted Samuel Johnson's words as a creed and they certainly describe it: "There is nothing which has yet been contrived by man by which so much happiness is produced as by a good inn." Dating back to the 1720s, the hotel retains its old-world charm with creaking wooden floorboards, polished tile floors, old prints, beams, ancient sofas covered in old-fashioned chintz, and antique furniture. The Gelletlie family has owned the inn since 1820, and now Tom and Richard Gelletlie (the fifth generation) ably assist their mother, Maureen. There is a delightful feeling of another age, which endures in the tradition of vast, Sunday roast lunches (1 pm prompt: book ahead) and afternoon teas of oven-fresh scones and strawberry jam—a particularly delightful feast when enjoyed in the garden on a warm summer's afternoon. You can sleep in bedrooms that kings have slept in—the king of Sweden has paid several visits. I loved my room 17 a spacious ground floor twin. Be sure to request a room with a view of the flower-filled gardens stretching beside the hotel down to the River Vartry. Some interesting gardens and houses are a short drive away: Powerscourt with its grand gardens, Mount Usher with its informal gardens, and Avondale House with its wooded parklands. *Directions:* Take the N11 from Dublin to Rathnew and turn left in the village for the 1-km drive to Hunters Hotel.

🛏️ 🧹 💳 ☎ @ P ⚑ ♿ ⚓ 🎣 🥾 🐎

HUNTER'S HOTEL
Owner: The Gelletlie family
Rathnew, Co Wicklow, Ireland
Tel: 040 440106, Fax: 040 440338
16 Rooms, Double: €190–€210
Dinner: from €48
Closed: Christmas, Credit cards: all major
Ireland's Blue Book
Inn

Tinakilly House maintains the purpose for which it was designed—gracious living. The house was built in the 1870s by Captain Robert Halpin, the commander of the ship Great Eastern, which laid the first telegraph cable connecting Europe to America. Tinakilly House's ornate staircase is reputed to be a copy of the one on this ship. Whether or not this is true is a matter of conjecture, but the Captain certainly spared no expense when he built this classical house with its fine, pitch-pine doors and shutters and ornate plasterwork ceilings. The original house has been extended with rooms that fit in perfectly. The house is furnished with appropriate Victorian furniture, and there's a welcoming charm to the place. Some of the bedrooms have four-poster beds, while all twenty junior suites and two captain suites have sea views. Dining is a delight. Tinakilly is an ideal countryside base for exploring Dublin, Glendalough, and the Wicklow Mountains. *Directions:* From Dublin take the N11 (Wexford road) to Rathnew village. Turn left, towards Wicklow, and the entrance to the hotel is on your left as you leave the village.

TINAKILLY HOUSE
Manager: Conrad Robinson
Rathnew, Co Wicklow, Ireland
Tel: 040 469274, Fax: 040 467806
21 Rooms, Double: €210–€263
30 Suites: €242–€336
Dinner: €65
Closed: Christmas, Credit cards: all major
Country House Hotel

Simon O'Hara is the seventh generation of his family to call Coopershill home since it was built in 1774. It is one of those wonderful places that offer the best of both worlds—the luxury of a country house hotel and the warmth of a home. You can even rent the entire place on a weekly basis for a house party. Simon welcome guests to his family home through the massive front door into the stove-warmed hall whose flagged floor is topped by an Oriental rug, and where rain gear hangs at the ready. Beyond lies a parade of lovely rooms tastefully decorated and beautifully furnished with grand, antique furniture, much of which is as old as the house itself. All but three of the bedrooms have the original four-poster or half-tester beds, but, of course, with modern mattresses. All the bedrooms are large and have private bathrooms. The only one with its bathroom down the hall requires an instruction manual to operate its magnificent shower! Ancestors' portraits gaze down upon you in the dining room, set with tables to accommodate individual parties. After an excellent dinner, guests chat round the fire over coffee. Secluded by 500 acres of farm and woodland, there are many delightful walks. Boating and fishing are available. There is enough sightseeing to justify spending a week here. *Directions:* From Dublin take the N4 to Drumfin (18 km south of Sligo). Turn right towards Riverstown and Coopershill is on your left 1 km before the village.

COOPERSHILL
Owner: The O'Hara family
Riverstown, Co Sligo, Ireland
Tel: 071 91 65108, Fax: 071 91 65466
8 Rooms, Double: €229–€285
1 House: €6000 weekly
Dinner: €62
Open: Apr to Oct, Credit cards: all major
Ireland's Blue Book
Country House & Self Catering

In summer, the driveway of Rosturk Woods is lined with wild red fuchsias that lead you to the low white house hugging a vast expanse of firm, sandy beach on the shores of Clew Bay. Home to Louisa and Alan Stoney and their young family (Alan grew up in the imposing castle next door, while Louisa's mother lives close by), the house has the feel of an old cottage, though it is only a few years old. Bedrooms have stripped-pine doors and several have pine-paneled, sloping ceilings. There's a lot of old pine furniture, antique pieces, and attractive prints and fabrics. The house cleverly divides so that a wing of two or three large bedrooms, a living room, and a kitchen can be closed off and used as self-catering accommodation. A delightful self-catering cottage has four beds and is equipped for handicapped guests. Louisa can sometimes direct you to nearby places where traditional Irish music is played. You can play tennis on the Stoneys' court, or hire their boat for a full- or half-day trip on Clew Bay. In contrast to the lush green fields and long sandy beaches that hug Clew Bay, a short drive brings you to the wilder, more rugged scenery of Achill Island. To the south lie Newport and Westport. *Directions:* From Westport take the N59 through Newport towards Achill Island. Before you arrive in Mulrany, cross the Owengarve river and after 500 meters turn left into the woodland to Rosturk Woods.

ROSTURK WOODS
Owners: Louisa & Alan Stoney
Rosturk
Mulrany, Co. Mayo, Ireland
Tel & Fax: 098 36264
3 Rooms, Double: €100–€150
1 Cottage: €750–€1500 weekly
Dinner: €40
Open: Feb to Nov, Credit cards: none
B&B & Self Catering

Built as a hotel in the 1880s, by a sea captain who also served as the local rector, Grove House has over the ensuing years attracted famous literati to the extent that Katarina Runske has named her rooms after them. Somerville and Ross (who wrote "The Irish R. M.") are two queen bedded rooms that look out across the garden to the water. Yeats (the famous painter and brother of the poet), Carberry, and Shaw are the most spacious; Shaw having the original loo in its bathroom. With only one bathroom in the house in times past it is fairly certain that all these men of letters used it. Dinner is a real treat cooked by Katarina, her mum and son Nico. Max, Katarina's other son, makes sure guests are well taken care of. Toast your toes by the fire in the sitting room and decide where you would like to go the next day. You'll be spoilt for choice: a ferry to the beautiful Cape Clear or Sherkin Island, a summer evening boat trip to Fasnet Island Lighthouse (Ireland's tallest most southerly lighthouse—the last piece of Ireland emigrants saw as they sailed for America), golf, walking, diving, or visiting scenic Mizen Head. *Directions:* The Mizen Peninsula is off N71 (Cork to Killarney road). Arriving is Schull turn left opposite the AIB into Colla Road and the house is about 500m on the right hand side.

GROVE HOUSE
Owners: Katarina Runske & Family
Colla Road
Schull, Co. Cork, Ireland
Tel: 028 28067, Fax: 028 28069
5 Rooms, Double: €100
Dinner: €25
Open: all year, Credit cards: all major
Country House

Ballymaloe House is a rambling, 17th-century manor house built onto an old Norman keep surrounded by lawns, a small golf course, and 400 acres of farmland. Run by members of the extended Allen family, Ballymaloe has established a reputation for outstanding hospitality and superb food, yet everything is decidedly informal. Families are made especially welcome (play equipment, outdoor heated pool in summer, childrens' meals) and several of the rooms can be linked together to accommodate them. Guests gather before dinner in the lounge to make their selections from the set menu, which offers four or five choices for each course. The bedrooms in the main house come in all shapes and sizes, from large and airy to cozy. For peace and quiet opt for one of the lovely garden rooms several of which have little patios and direct access to the garden. Surrounding a courtyard, the smaller stable bedrooms offer country-cottage charm—and beamed ceilings for those on the upper floor. Blarney and Kinsale are within easy striking distance but allow time to play a game of croquet, go for a walk or a bike ride; and explore the coast with its small rocky inlets, fishing harbors, and lonely headlands. Need a gift there's no need to go further than the car park where the Ballymaloe shop offers the best of all-things Irish. *Directions:* Ballymaloe is signposted from the N25 (Cork to Waterford road)—3 km beyond Cloyne on the Ballycotton Road.

BALLYMALOE HOUSE
Manager: Hazel Allen
Shanagarry
Midleton, Co. Cork, Ireland
Tel: 021 4652531, Fax: 021 4652021
33 Rooms, Double: €110–€200
5 Cottages: €500 weekly
Dinner: €75
Closed: Dec 24 to 27, Credit cards: all major
Ireland's Blue Book
Country House Hotel & Self Catering

The K Club began life as The Kildare Hotel & Country Club but as everyone shortened the name, they changed it. Stay here and you get preference for tee times on the championship golf courses designed by Arnold Palmer. If you do intend to play, enquire about the golf packages that include accommodation and green fees. Even if you are not a golfer, this is the most sumptuous of places to stay—the grandest of houses with a parade of luxurious, beautiful rooms. The artwork is exquisite, with a room devoted to Jack Yeats's paintings. Taking pride of place in the magnificent dining room is The Byerly Turk, a massive 17th-century portrait of one of the three stallions that sired every thoroughbred in the world. Fine cooking is an essential ingredient here and the menu includes Irish classics such as roast Wicklow lamb as well as more nirvana-like fare. Pamper yourself in the health spa, splash in the pool, or just stroll through the acres of gardens and revel in the sheer luxury of the place. Exquisite self-catering apartments are available. It is easy to understand why The K Club represents an ideal of luxury for so many people. *Directions:* Take the N7 (Kildare road) out of Dublin to Kill where you turn right for the 5-km drive to The K Club, on your left just before Straffan.

THE K CLUB
Manager: Michael Davern
Straffan, Co Kildare, Ireland
Tel: 01 6017200, Fax: 01 6017299
58 Rooms, Double: €280–€625
11 Suites: €575–€7000
24 Apartments: €675 daily
Dinner: €65–€75
Open: all year, Credit cards: all major
Ireland's Blue Book
Luxury Resort & Self Catering

I arrived on a windswept stormy day to be revived by hot tea and a slice of cake. The journey was quickly forgotten as I became engrossed in Patricia's tale of training the new rooster to begin his song at 8 am, instead of dawn, to give guests a good lie in. Patricia and her husband Austin (passionate about all-things golf) are welcoming hosts, generous with their time and experts at planning trips—one along the coast and across the little ferry to Waterford is a favorite with guests. Their farmhouse dates back to 1703 and over the years various owners have made additions and changes with, most recently, Austin and Patricia's transformation. Incredibly, the soaring garden room, where you toast your toes before the fire and gather for sherry before dinner, was recently a crumbling piggery. Bedrooms come in all shapes and sizes are priced accordingly. Patricia's dinner celebrates good country food with local, organic produce. Austin offers a short, value-for-money, wine list. If you are traveling to Ireland via the Rosslare Ferry, a stay at here is an excellent introduction to Ireland or a great place to spend your last nights in the Emerald Isle. *Directions:* Tagoat is on the N25, 6 km north of Rosslare harbor. Turn between the church and pub onto R736. Churchtown House is on your left after 1 km.

CHURCHTOWN HOUSE
Owners: Patricia & Austin Cody
Tagoat
Rosslare, Co. Wexford, Ireland
Tel: 053 9132555, Fax: 053 9132577
12 Rooms, Double: €120–€150
Dinner: €40 (not Sun or Mon)
Open: Mar 1 to Nov 1, Credit cards: all major
Country House

Tir Na Fiúise offers you a perfect base for exploring the mid-west and Shannon region. Inez and Niall Heenan have converted the barns just down the lane from their farmhouse to self-catering accommodation rented by the week. The delightful cottages are decorated with a simple, fresh, country look. The kitchen/living areas feature solid-fuel stoves and modern appliances such as dishwashers and microwaves. The Hawthorns is a one- or two-bedroom cottage with king-sized beds. The Granary is a one-bedroom cottage just perfect for a couple getting away from it all to a cozy little nook, while The Stables has two bedrooms, making it more suitable for a family or larger group. The Lime Kiln also has two bedrooms and is larger than the Stables. The area has some excellent restaurants and local pubs, which also serve great food. Inez and Niall encourage guests to explore their organic farm and adjacent bog land. You can cycle along the quiet lanes, try your hand at fishing in the nearby lough, and join in village activities. On Thursday nights, May to September, there is Irish music and dance in the village hall. If you must rush off to tourist spots, Bunratty Folk Park is a 90-minute drive away (as is Shannon airport). Closer at hand are Clonmacnois and Birr Castle. *Directions:* Leave the N7 in Nenagh and travel through Borrisokane and Ballinderry to Terryglass. The lane leading to Tir Na Fiúise (1 km on your left) is opposite the bridge in the village.

TIR NA FIÚISE
Owners: Inez & Niall Heenan
Terryglass
Nenagh, Co. Tipperary, Ireland
Tel & Fax: 067 22041
4 Cottages: €280–€980 weekly
Open: all year, Credit cards: MC, VS
Self Catering

Only in Ireland can you have a village that does not exist! Inch House is the only building in Inch while the nearest village, Bouladuff, is known and signposted only as "The Ragg" in spite of being marked as Bouladuff on maps—hence we list Inch House under Thurles! Follow the directions and you'll reach this stately Georgian home surrounded by miles of farmland. The house was built in 1720 by the Ryan family. Nora and John Egan originally came here to farm with their eight children who are now grown. Daughter Maureen works closely with her parents and chances are you'll meet one or two of the other children around the place. It's a real treat to stay here for it is quintessentially Irish and incredibly homey in spite of having ballroom-sized drawing and dining rooms resplendent with 15-foot-high ceilings. Michael Galvin is in charge of the kitchen and his set dinner menu (plenty of choices for each course) focuses on local produce. A grand sweep of polished oak stairs lead up to the bedrooms where room 26 is large enough to hold a party, room 24 has a stupendous half-tester bed, and room 27 offers a four-poster. Cashel with its famous rock is a half-hour drive away. *Directions:* From the N8 (Dublin to Cork road) take the turnoff to Thurles. Go to the town square and take the Nenagh road for 6 km past "The Ragg" and the driveway to the house is on your left.

INCH HOUSE
Owners: Nora & John Egan
Thurles, Co Tipperary, Ireland
Tel: 050 451348, Fax: 050 451754
5 Rooms, Double: €130–€150
Dinner: €60 (not Sun or Mon)
Closed: Christmas & Easter, Credit cards: MC, VS
Country House

Fortview house is a traditional stone built, slate roofed, Irish farmhouse that has been thoughtfully expanded. Full of antiques, collectibles, quiet nooks, pine floors and exposed beams, it hunkers down next to the country road, sheltering from the prevailing wind off the not-too-distant Atlantic Ocean. Richard works the farm and guests are welcome to visit and learn the intricacies of dairy herd management first hand. Violet pours heart and soul into operating the bed and breakfast. Five country-comfortable rooms with brass beds and small, but well equipped en-suite bathrooms, are all named after local flowers. An airy conservatory provides guests with a sunny spot to relax with a cup of tea or coffee. Breakfast is served in the dining room with its rough-wood mantled brick fireplace and its black iron stove. A large pine country dresser, matching chairs and tables covered in blue and white checkered table cloths complete the scene. In addition to your cooked breakfast there will be local cheese, home made jams, fresh baked bread, scones and hot croissants to accompany, fresh squeezed juice, compote and potato cakes with crème fraiche and fresh salmon. Drive West Cork's peninsulas: Mizzen Head, Sheeps Head and the Beara Peninsula; visit Bantry House and Glengarrif Island; and take the ferry to Cape Clear. *Directions:* Located 2km from Toormore on the road to Durrus. (R591). Fortview House is 12km from Durrus and 9km from Goleen.

FORTVIEW HOUSE
Owners: Violet & Richard Connell
Gurtyowen
Toormore
Goleen, Co. Cork, Ireland
Tel & Fax: 028 35324
5 Rooms, Double: €100
1 House: €400–€950 weekly
Open: all year, Credit cards: none
B&B & Self Catering

Ardtara, a grand home with well-proportioned rooms and lovely stained-glass windows, was built in 1856 by the Clark family, owners of the village linen mill. A downturn in the Clark family fortunes shut the gates for many years, and the house lay sleeping until it received a new lease on life as a country house hotel. Central heating and modern bathrooms were added, but care was taken in keeping architectural details. Many of the 16 original fireplaces have been converted to open gas fires, which give the house a cheerful warmth. All but one of the bedrooms has a cozy fireplace. It's a comfortable place where the staff, many are locals, offers a warmth welcome. The restaurant has gained an excellent reputation for his food and takes great pride in his locally sourced produce. The impressive dining room has a hunting frieze and a ceiling dominated by an enormous glass skylight, a perfect place to enjoy Monica's food. Just a 5 minutes drive from major roads, Ardtara is a perfect location for a day trip along the Antrim coast to visit the famous Giant's Causeway. Derry town is an hour's drive away and guests often take a guided walk around the city walls. *Directions:* From Belfast take the M2 motorway to A6 (Londonderry road). After Castledawson, take A29 towards Coleraine. Just beyond Maghera, turn right at the Upperlands and Kilrea signpost. Go through the village of Upperlands. The hotel is on your left.

ARDTARA COUNTRY HOUSE
Manager: Valerie Ferson
8 Gorteade Road
Upperlands, BT46 5SA, Northern Ireland
Tel: 028 796 44490, Fax: 028 796 45080
9 Rooms, Double: £180
Dinner: £30
Open: all year, Credit cards: all major
Country House Hotel

Foxmount is the sort of house that feels like home from the moment you walk in the front door. David and Margaret have been taking guests on their family farm for over forty years, and they very much enjoy welcoming guests from all parts of the world to enjoy the homely comforts and experiences of a family run country house on a working farm. Margaret is a natural at hospitality while David loves to talk about the farm and give advice on what to do and see in the area—the Waterford crystal factory is a big draw. Margaret feeds her guests lavish breakfasts. Tasty porridge cooked on the Aga with lots of cream. Scones that melt in your mouth with lashings of raspberry jam. Walk up the garden and see the fruits that she uses: strawberries, raspberries, gooseberries, apples, and rhubarb fresh from the garden. There's no shortage of places to go for dinner and you are welcome to relax and make yourself at home in the drawing room. Upstairs, the extremely comfortable bedrooms have very nice bathrooms—two with showers over the tub and two with their shower cubicles tucked into separate little closets. One has an extra bed, making it ideal for families. Just down the road is the Passage East Ferry which takes you across the river to the pretty Hook peninsula. *Directions:* Take the road from Waterford toward Dunmore East. Three km after passing the hospital, take the left fork toward Passage East. Foxmount Farms is signposted on the right after 500 meters.

▰ 🚵 @ W P 🏃 ⛵ 🧍 🏇 🏄

FOXMOUNT FARMS COUNTRY HOUSE
Owners: Margaret & David Kent
Passage East Road
Waterford, Co Waterford, Ireland
Tel: 051 874308, Fax: 051 854906
4 Rooms, Double: €130
Open: Mar to Oct, Credit cards: none
Country House

Youghal (pronounced "you all" with an American southern drawl), a workaday fishing port, is beginning to flaunt its historic past: drab, gray buildings are being restored, empty shopfronts are coming to life. Standing amongst them, Aherne's old-world pub exterior is decked out in shiny new paint. Owned by the Fitzgibbon family since 1923, Aherne's includes a seafood restaurant and bedrooms. There's an old-world, traditional atmosphere in the bars where you can enjoy a pint with the locals and an array of tempting bar food. The restaurant specializes in locally caught seafood and the menu changes daily, depending on what is fresh and available. In the guests' sitting room, a cozy fire is flanked by comfortable sofas and a coffee table stacked with books on all-things Irish. Three ground-floor bedrooms offer easy access, with one specially equipped for wheelchairs. I particularly enjoyed the upstairs rooms, which have little balconies facing the courtyard. All guestrooms have attractive decor, antique furniture, and large firm beds, each accompanied by an immaculate bathroom. For a stay of longer than a couple of nights the Fitzgibbons have two studio apartments adjacent to the hotel and a luxurious, two-bedroom penthouse apartment with breathtaking views of the harbor. *Directions:* Youghal is between Waterford and Cork on the N25. Aherne's is on the main street in town.

≗ ⚒ 💳 ☎ @ W P ⫽ ⊘ 🎨 🐾 ⚿ 🏊 ☂ 🚶 ⛷ 🏇

AHERNE'S
Owners: Gaye, Kate, John & David Fitzgibbon
163 North Main Street
Youghal, Co Cork, Ireland
Tel: 024 92424, Fax: 024 93633
10 Rooms, Double: €170–€240, 3 Suites: €220–€300
3 Apartments: €400–€1800 weekly
Dinner: €48
Closed: Christmas, Credit cards: all major
Ireland's Blue Book
Restaurant With Rooms & Self Catering

Index

Index

KAREN BROWN wrote her first travel guide in 1976. Her personalized travel series has grown to 17 titles, which Karen and her small staff work diligently to keep updated. Karen, her husband, Rick, and their children, Alexandra and Richard, live in a small town on the coast south of San Francisco.

JUNE EVELEIGH BROWN hails from Sheffield, England and lived in Zambia and Canada before moving to northern California where she lives in San Mateo with her husband, Tony, their German Shepherd, and a Siamese cat.

BARBARA MACLURCAN TAPP draws all of the delightful hotel sketches and illustrations in this guide. Barbara was raised in Sydney, Australia, where she studied interior design. Although she continues with architectural rendering and watercolor painting, she devotes much of her time to illustrating the Karen Brown guides. Barbara lives in Kensington, California, with her husband, Richard, and is Mum to Jono, Alex and Georgia. For more information about her work visit *www.barbaratapp.com.*

JANN POLLARD, the artist of the all the beautiful cover paintings in the Karen Brown series, has studied art since childhood and is well known for her outstanding impressionistic-style watercolors. Jann has received numerous achievement awards and her works are in private and corporate collections internationally. She is also a popular workshop teacher in the United States, Mexico and Europe. *www.jannpollard.com.* Fine art giclée prints of her paintings are available at *www.karenbrown.com.*